To my mother- and father-in-law,
Julia and Joseph 'Butch' Revai

Table of Contents

Acknowledgements

I met a lot of wonderful people in the process of writing this book—in person, via e-mail, through snail mail and phone calls—and I owe each of them a debt of gratitude for their assistance. So my deepest thanks go to the following contributors, whose stories, photographs, and 'permissions-to-use' make up this book:

In alphabetical order—A Step Above Hair Studio; Amanda Armstrong; Murray Armstrong; Teresa Bender and family; Grace Bergman; Jennifer B.; Lois Caskinett; Cheryl; Stephanie and Matthew Comini; Rick Dalrymple; David; Noah Flint; Jared Greene; Tom Griffis; Venna Hillman; Hillary Littlejohn; Linda Marshall; Maureen and Jared McCargar; Teresa Mitchell; Janis Monroe; Heather Montford; Lauren Mulvaugh; Joshua Murphy; Nickie Neil; Grand Lodge of New York—IOOF; Olivia; Paraphysical Studies and Investigations (PSI); Bud and Bev Perry; Connie Repas; Melodie Rogers; Nikki Rogers; Janet Rutigliano; Nickki Ryan; Belle and Gary Salisbury; Robyn Sawyer and family; Jon Scheer; Lawrence Scheer; Seaway Trail Discovery Center; Tim Stevens; Barry Strate; Eileen Strate; Terry; Terry; Todd; Watertown City School District; Peggy Neil West; Laura and John Whalen; and Sandra Wyman.

I'd like to thank Theresa Sharp (Town of Massena historian) and all town and village historians who offered their support in one way or another in the development of this series. They are excellent resources, and we should appreciate their voluntary efforts.

Much gratitude goes to Sheila Orlin, Rob Igoe, Zach Steffen, and the entire staff at North Country Books, Inc. Their guidance and expertise are invaluable, and it's always a pleasure working with them. Many thanks also to Leland Farnsworth for his invaluable support and encouragement and to Judy Farnsworth and Pendra King—two special ladies whose friendships I hold dear. Most of all, I thank my family, Joe, Michelle, Jamie, Katie, and Nikki; my parents, Tom and Jean Dishaw; my siblings, Tom Dishaw, Christina Walker, and Cindy Barry; and my in-laws, Joseph 'Butch' and Julia Revai. I thank God for my family.

Introduction

Not long ago, genuine spirit photographs seemed a prized rarity and, by comparison, ghost stories were fairly easy to come by. Today, the number of spirit photographs being taken is fast approaching the number of new ghost stories surfacing, and both can be found in abundance. That's why "Dying to Be Seen" is a theme whose time has come. With a seemingly unlimited number of photographs and ghost stories at my disposal, I'm able to offer an accurate depiction of what ghosts and spirits really look like, using photographic examples and detailed personal accounts that thoroughly describe close encounters of the paranormal kind. In this third installment of the Haunted Northern New York series, both picture lovers and story lovers alike will find something to satisfy their passion for ghosts.

Some of the images of ghosts in this book are so obvious that they seem to jump right off the page at us. But ghosts can't jump off pages— or can they? I had one person renege on showing me her ghost photograph, because of the odd things that started happening to her once she decided to 'go public' with her strange picture. Whatever was in that photograph must have been convincing enough that she didn't want to take any chances on upsetting 'It.'

Usually spirit energy on film is so vague that a person can get frown lines from squinting to see it, zooming in and pouring over every last pixel, or leaning in for a closer look at the actual photograph with a magnifying glass. I'm speaking from experience here.

For the most part, defining spirit energy is an imprecise art. It takes some practice to know what you're looking for and to recognize it when you see it. After all, we're talking about ghosts. They're not solid like you or I, so we can't expect them to appear as such.

There are legions of spirit beings among us waiting to be noticed. There always have been, and there always will be. Ghost stories and spirit photographs are nothing new. The only thing new today is the sheer *volume* of stories and pictures. Everyone knows someone who knows someone who has seen a ghost or taken a 'really weird photograph.' But spirit images on film really haven't changed that much. Ghosts showed up in old-time black and white or sepia photographs as semi-transparent faces and full-bodied apparitions that didn't belong, just as they do today. But we now have the ability to capture many more types of spirit energy on film; and when we do, we have the means to analyze it, enhance it, and confirm its authenticity.

The following example of a genuine antique spirit photograph was provided by Sandra Wyman, Town of Rossie Historian. It's called "Bird's Eye View of Rossie, N.Y.," and it dates to around 1903. Not only did the photographer capture the essence of Rossie; he inadvertently captured a crafty ghost, as well. The postcard is shown in its entirety in *More*

Photo courtesy of Sandra Wyman

Grinning face in foreground appears out of nowhere, Rossie, c 1903

Haunted Northern New York, but for our purposes here, it's been cropped and enlarged so you can easily spot the grinning ghost face that appears out of nowhere between the photographer and the nearest building.

Ghost stories will always be of interest, as well. They caused as much excitement in the distant past as they do today. Take the following article from *The Heuvelton Bee* in 1902 as an example:

"HEUVELTON—We occasionally read of ghosts and haunted houses away off in other parts of the world, but Heuvelton and vicinity, not to be outdone, has one of their own. The house is on the Irish Settlement Road where mysterious things occur, and at least two families have felt obliged to leave the house because of what they claim to have heard or seen. You cannot make them believe [in ghosts] but that they have seen the spirit of a woman at different times, and the peculiar and unaccounted for noises they have heard on several occasions have nearly frightened them out of their wits. So much has been said about the matter that some are proposing to investigate." (A paranormal investigation in 1902? Now *that* would have been something!)

Much has changed, and yet much remains the same. Ghosts and spirits still look and act the same as they always have, and people still fearfully flee their homes and call priests and investigators in to assist. But in 1902, local people often hushed their own experiences for fear of ridicule, wrongly assuming that ghosts were more a product of far-off, distant lands. In 2004, we know better. There are haunted places everywhere, equally distributed around the globe. Ghosts don't discriminate —wherever people are, ghosts will be.

Because of an increasing acceptance of paranormal phenomena, most people today no longer fear mockery for their beliefs in the supernatural. Indeed, ghost-hunting has become the in-thing. As a result, paranormal investigation is a booming business.

Preface

Dying to Be Seen

With today's technology, we do seem to be capturing spirit energy on film far more often than we did in the past. Cameras "see" differently than the human eye does, just as animals and insects see differently than we do. High-speed, high-definition film and state-of-the-art equipment allows us to compensate for the physical limitations of our vision. The camera lens takes over where our senses leave off, providing us with a different view of our surroundings—and of its less conspicuous occupants.

However, complex equipment in the field of photography cannot be given full credit for the upsurge in spirit photographs taken these days, though it certainly seems to help. But more and more people are finding evidence of spirit activity in photographs they've taken with simple instant cameras, disposable cameras, digital cameras, and other very basic photographic equipment. People browsing through stacks and shoeboxes of family photos are also finding more images of spirits than they did years ago. I think this is simply because people have become increasingly aware of what to look for and what constitutes spirit energy in photographs. Most people are quite surprised (and either frightened or delighted) to see the unexplainable images they've captured in their photographs. The standard remark is, "I'm sure it wasn't there when I took the photograph." But there it is, plain as day. By the time you finish reading this book, I guarantee you'll look at your own pictures differently in the future.

Spirit energy takes many forms, and below I'll describe the more common ways they manifest—supported by remarkable photographs taken by several North Country residents. As the number of genuine spirit photographs continues to multiply—and make no mistake, it *is* multiplying—we are becoming more adept at categorizing and classifying what we find. The results are astounding, but the field of paranormal research is yet so new that we have barely begun to realize the many ways spirit can be discerned: orbs, spirit mist, apparitions.

Orbs

Orbs are simply balls of spirit energy that move about unfettered and easily. Imagine our very essence all compressed into a little sphere of pulsating energy. An orb is said to be the most basic form that a spirit can present itself in, and it is the first step one would take toward apparitional manifestation. Orbs are just the beginning. They are to apparitions what embryos are to full-term infants—the simple to the very complex.

The most frequently seen spirit phenomenon today, orbs appear as globes of light that can range from being fully transparent to being brilliant, opaque spheres. Based on the many photographs I've seen, the most common color of an orb is white, but other colors are often seen as well. People who have seen orbs in person often report 'strings' of orbs floating across a room or groups of them flitting about. Some even appear to have faces in them, as in the following example.

Melodie Rogers took the following photograph at the Massena

Photo by Melodie Rogers

Cemetery orb with face, Massena

Center Cemetery. She was using a digital camera. She told me, "I never had so many appear at once, ever."

"I was with my stepdaughter, Nikki, and it was only seven o'clock or so, but it was a very dark night. In fact, I looked up into the sky, and there wasn't a star to be seen—or even the moon. I had, at one point, hesitated about even going, because it was so dark. We walked back into the older part, and it was so black that we could barely see where we were walking. I started taking random pictures, because I literally couldn't see anything at all, not even the gravestones. I took about twenty or so pictures and told Nikki I was ready to go, because it was way too creepy. I took one more picture, and just before I snapped the button, I saw a huge glow in front of my eyes. It scared the heck out of me, and I said, 'That's it! We're leaving, *now*!' We ran to the car, which seemed miles away, but it was only a few hundred feet. Like I said, *never* had I actually seen anything while taking pictures in cemeteries, until that night. When we got home, we downloaded the pictures onto the computer, and, sure enough, that's when we saw the orb with the face. The other pictures were full of orbs, too, but nothing as prominent as that one."

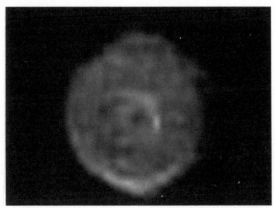

Photo by Melodie Rogers
Close-up of cemetery orb showing face, Massena

Certain conditions, such as dust particles, water droplets, snowflakes, or even insects, can mimic the appearance of orbs in photographs. Experienced paranormal researchers and photographers are careful to avoid and rule out any such false positives.

Photo by Melodie Rogers

Perfect example of an orb at Massena Center Cemetery, Massena

Spirit Mist

Spirit mist—also known as ecto-mist, ghost mist, ghost fog, etc.—is yet another form that spirit energy takes. Based on our knowledge of this phenomenon, it seems to be somewhere between the orb and the final apparitional form. It appears in various colors, most often red or white, and may look like rays of colored light (sometimes called 'sprites') that shoot upward. Occasionally, there are several different types of spirit mist in the same photograph, as well as several types of spirit energy.

Belle Salisbury, owner of The Whispering Willow metaphysical shop and spiritual learning center in Sandy Creek, is a gifted psychic who does—among many things—home investigations for people experiencing paranormal activity. She provided me with several photos to use, including the following three examples of spirit mist.

The first photograph was taken by Belle from inside her house during a snowfall at her home in Sandy Creek. The house was left to her husband Gary when his father passed away. Gary was shoveling—you can barely make out his legs in the dark background—and Belle was watching him. The snow in front of Gary forms a mist that clearly looks like a man turned sideways holding the shovel and helping Gary dig!

Perhaps it was his father pitching in. I wasn't sure whether to put this one in the mist or apparition category, because it's somewhere between the two. Whatever it is, it's one of my favorites.

Photo by Belle Salisbury
Snow spirit, Sandy Creek

The next two photographs were taken at Belle's and Gary's "Civil War wedding" in Rochester on Halloween of 1999. The first shows a sprite of energy parallel to a genuine Civil War rifle held by her son, Rickey, on the left side of the photo. The energy is red in the actual color photograph.

Photo provided by Belle Salisbury
Ray of spirit energy along Civil War rifle, Rochester

The second photo shows spirit energy (again red) coming out of one of the old nunnery's windows during the ceremony, as well as spirit energy directly behind the first person sitting in the last row, and yet more spirit energy in the upper left-hand corner. But that's not all. In the second-floor window, furthest to the right, it looks like a face is gazing out toward the trees (a very prominent face, perhaps of a Civil War soldier). The window to the left of it also appears to have a possible apparition of a figure from the chest up to the jaw line. This photograph is oozing with spirit energy. What a wonderful Halloween wedding surprise for Belle and Gary!

Photo provided by Belle Salisbury

Spirit energy at nunnery, Rochester

As with orbs, there are certain conditions that might cause a false image of spirit mist in photographs. Smoking is forbidden when taking paranormal photographs, because the white, swirling smoke can be mistaken for spirit energy. If it's cold enough to see your breath, you would consider either holding your breath or covering your mouth and nose while taking the photograph. The vapor from your breath could appear as potential spirit energy. Light reflections, sunlight streaming through trees directly overhead, and faulty or old film should always be ruled out, as they were in the photographs shown above. Belle's wedding day was cloudy with no sunlight.

Apparitions

An apparition is spirit energy that clearly takes on an animal or human form. It is the rarest and most exciting type of spirit energy to capture on film, perhaps due to the immense effort (on the spirit's part) that we believe is required to morph from an orb into a mist, and finally, into an apparition. Apparitions can be nearly invisible outlines of people, faces, and animals, or completely solid-looking beings-and anything in-between. They may appear to be black, white, or grayish, in full color, or as a colorless vapor with a defined outline. Occasionally, they are surrounded by light.

Melodie Rogers captured the following apparition on film in a cemetery in Fort Covington. She pointed the camera in the direction of a pile of rubble and a couple of gravestones. When she got the film developed, she was surprised to see an apparition in the woods *behind* the cemetery. In the upper edge of the photograph, just behind the brush line is a mysterious figure, seen from the shoulders up, standing beside a tree. The man seems to have an eerie glow about him.

Photo by Melodie Rogers

Figure in the bushes, Fort Covington

A few weeks later, Mel visited the same cemetery, snapping pictures at random objects. She didn't expect that her spooky visitor from the last time would make another appearance, but he did. This time, he was in a different part of the graveyard—again peeking out from the bushes and only appearing from the shoulders up (just left of the center of the photo). In this photo, his head and shoulders have the same peculiar glow that the man in the first photograph had. We have no idea who the ghost could be, but he made quite an impression on Mel. His presence in her photos was disturbing enough that she based her first horror novel on him!

Photo by Melodie Rogers

Another presence in the woods, Fort Covington

The investigative team that was introduced in *More Haunted Northern New York*, Paraphysical Studies and Investigations (PSI), provided me with an incredible example of an apparition from a very haunted home in Binghamton that they investigated. The following photograph was taken by a person who lived there. While the photographer walked through the house taking pictures, his daughter sat quietly at the dining room table, coloring. But the photograph clearly shows *two* little girls sitting at the table. One of them didn't belong—the girl on the right—and nobody knows who she was or why she was there; but she certainly wasn't there when the photograph was taken.

Photo courtesy of PSI

Little girl with unknown company (right), Binghamton

It looks like the ghost child is wearing an unusual hat or has her hair pulled up into a pointed bun and is just watching the 'real' little girl, who seemed entirely unaware of her ghostly visitor. Much of the photo is distorted, which is common in spirit photography. In fact, sometimes you end up with nothing but a blur of colorful strings of light throughout a picture, because of the immense spirit energy present at the time it was taken. At any rate, because of all the distortion in this photograph, the apparition stands out better when viewed in negative mode below.

Photo courtesy of PSI

Negative of little girl with unknown company, Binghamton

Ralph Waldo Emerson (1803-1882) said, "Nature always wears the colors of the spirit." How true. Remember Belle Salisbury's "Snow Spirit" photograph from earlier? That was a perfect example. The last photograph of an apparition in this section also illustrates how well ghosts can (and do) camouflage themselves in nature. Melodie Rogers took this picture of her step-daughter, Nikki, who thought she was onto something in the spot where she was playfully standing and pointing. Unbeknownst to the two of them, the real spirit was actually watching them from behind! On the right edge of the photograph, peeking out between two branches, you can clearly see a face.

Photo by Melodie Rogers

Watch out behind you! Fort Covington

Melodie Rogers has taken some truly spectacular ghost photographs in cemeteries, and Belle Salisbury has taken equally astounding photographs at private residences. My point is, it's important to understand that ghost pictures can be taken *anywhere*. Ghosts are as likely to be found in the old bedrooms they once slept in as they are on the sacred grounds where they were laid to their final rest. So pick up your cameras wherever you are and practice random acts of picture-taking. There's no question that someone, somewhere out there, is *dying to be seen*. The only question is, are you ready to see?

Close-up of apparition in branches, Fort Covington

Do Not Stand At My Grave

Do not stand at my grave and weep;
I am not there. I do not sleep.
I am the thousand winds that blow.
I am in the diamond glint on snow.
I am the sunlight on ripened grain.
I am the gentle autumn rain.
When you awaken in the morning's hush,
I am the swift uplifting rush
Of quiet birds in the circled flight.
I am the soft stars that shine at night.
Do not stand at my grave and cry;
I am not there. I did not die.

—Author Unknown

Ghost Sense

Watertown

Somewhere on the Sulphur Springs Road between Sackets Harbor and Watertown—but a bit closer to Watertown—sits an old house on a hill that was built in the 1890s. It's one of those places you can tell is haunted just by looking at it. But, since this story is anonymous, I can't show you a picture! However, I *can* give you an idea of what it's like to live there, from conversations with one who *did* and one who *does*.

Janis and Terry grew up in this house and wanted to share their experiences with me. Both have found that their heightened "spirit sense" that was nurtured and developed in their childhood home has only improved over the years. Though Terry no longer lives there, Janis does.

Terry's first experience was when he was just four or five years old. He set his favorite toy—a cap gun—down on a shelf one day when he was finished playing with it. He clearly remembered where he left it— between his mother's sewing room and the dining room. But the next day, it was missing. He asked his mother where it was, and she said she didn't know. "Maybe a ghost took it," she teased. Terry didn't even know what a ghost was, but he took her word for it. Two days later the cap gun reappeared in the exact spot he'd left it. Isn't that just like a ghost? Not frightening stuff, just typical mischievous behavior. Yet, it was a mild omen of more frightening things to come.

Janis was about five when she saw her first spirit, but she had a feeling something was there long before she ever actually saw it. Her family had gone to town for the evening, to a church gathering, and Janis, the youngest of six, was left home with a babysitter (her sister Mary's boyfriend). When it came time for bed, he told her to go upstairs and put on her pajamas. Like every child that age, the idea of getting ready for bed didn't particularly excite her, so she hemmed and hawed. But, *unlike* most children, she was stalling because she was afraid to go upstairs alone. She couldn't say why. She only knew that the air seemed to change and become dark and scary whenever she opened the door to go up the stairway to the second floor. Mary's boyfriend finally convinced her to go up and get her pajamas on, in case her parents came home early. So off she went.

Her heart was racing as she searched for the white cord that turned on the hallway light. *Will I get the light turned on before something reaches out of the dark and grabs me?* That's what she was thinking. Thankfully, the light came on—it always did—and she ran up the stairs as fast as she could into her room. *Safe at last.* She was digging frantically through her closet for her pajamas when she heard a noise behind her. She turned to see an old woman sitting in the wooden rocking chair in her room. The spirit's white hair was pulled up in a bun, and she was knitting. A full-grown cat that was at her feet jumped up into her lap, and the woman stopped knitting to stroke it. It was every bit a perfectly normal scene. And yet, it was all wrong. Realizing this, Janis opened her mouth to scream, but the old woman lifted a crooked finger to her lips in a hushing motion. She smiled at the frightened girl, and when Janis realized she wasn't going to be hurt, she smiled back—with all the innocence of a trusting child. Then the apparition faded—both the woman and the cat—and Janis ran downstairs to tell the babysitter what had happened. He let the distraught youngster stay with him until her parents returned home.

A short time later, Janis again found herself confronted by someone who didn't belong in her room, but these intruders were definitely planning to hurt someone! Not long after she'd gone to bed, she heard footsteps coming up the stairs toward her room. Her bed was positioned so that her head was near the door. The two people coming up the stairs were men, and they were talking about their intention to kill a little girl—*she was a little girl*! Janis could tell when they had reached her doorway. She felt paralyzed, but when she tried to scream out to her mother she was unable to make a sound, or even open her eyes. Her

2

entire body was too tense to even move.

Then she heard two other voices—those of a man and a woman. She finally managed to open her eyes and saw that they were dressed in white; but she could only see their heads and shoulders. She wasn't afraid of these two people at all. She believes that the white beings were angels trying to calm her down and let her know that she wouldn't be hurt by the two apparent thugs, who were ghosts. Once she calmed down enough for her throat muscles to relax, she felt a "high-pitched, ear-piercing scream that made everyone rise ten feet off their beds" escape her lungs.

In 1993 Janis, then going on twelve, moved into Becky's room, when Becky moved out. She had heard her sister's horror stories about the room, but she found them hard to believe, even though she had experienced some pretty bizarre things herself. It didn't take long after moving into the room before her tune quickly changed and she conceded that Becky hadn't been exaggerating! On many nights, Janis heard footsteps coming up the stairs and stopping just outside her bedroom door, which she compulsively locked each night. Whenever the footsteps reached her door, the doorknob began to rattle like someone was trying to get in, even though Janis knew everyone else was already in bed. She held her breath until the rattling stopped and waited for the footsteps to continue on to Terry's room, which was right next to hers.

Several years later Janis was talking to her niece and nephew, who were staying in an adjoining bedroom. They were in their beds talking in the dark. Suddenly, her niece and nephew called out to her with urgency. They were obviously frightened by something that was happening in their room. Janis knew the voice of fear. She jumped out of bed and ran in to help the youngsters with whatever it was. She sat on one of their beds just as the whole room began to spin. Neither of the children could move without feeling like they would fall over. Janis said, "We couldn't make anything out. The room was nothing but a huge, black blur with pinholes of light that were hardly visible. The room wouldn't stop moving, and the three of us screamed out for help. As soon as one of my sisters opened the bedroom door, the spinning stopped, and we told her what happened." Luckily, it was an isolated event. It was almost as if a portal had opened up for a few moments before slamming shut again.

3

Terry also recalls the rattling doorknobs, but he has a different story. He said his aunt was living with them for a time before she died, and her cat always rattled the upstairs doorknobs after she went to bed, because it wanted to be with her. A sweet, yet irritating, habit. The cat died of rabies, leaving Terry's aunt heartbroken. One night, after his aunt had passed on, Terry was the last one to go upstairs to bed. His head had just hit the pillow when he heard footsteps coming up the stairs. They stopped at the top of the stairs, and then the doorknob began to rattle incessantly, just as it had when that crazy cat was alive. No way was Terry about to get out of bed to see what it was. And if it wasn't the cat, he sure as heck didn't want to know who or what else it could possibly be! Hearing footsteps coming up the stairs was bad enough, but having your doorknob rattled was getting personal!

The next time Terry heard the mysterious footsteps was a few years later, when he was home alone. His parents and the rest of the family had gone on vacation for a week, leaving him to watch their house and keep an eye on his grandmother, who lived nearby. For the first couple of days, Terry was having a good a time with the house to himself and his family away on vacation. He was a teenager—need I say more? But then something happened that effectively changed his mind. A powerful thunderstorm passed through the area on his third night alone, but finally the winds subsided and the rain stopped. All was calm and quiet...too quiet. Nonetheless, Terry climbed into bed, turned off the radio and the light, and tucked himself in.

Suddenly, in the dead silence of the night, he heard footsteps downstairs heading toward the door to the upstairs. He tensed and pulled the blankets tighter until all that remained exposed was his head. He listened as the door to the upstairs opened, and the footsteps began their threatening ascent, slowly and heavily. When they reached the landing at the top of the stairs, Terry braced himself. *It had to be a ghost!* He heard the footsteps turn left, walk straight toward his bedroom door, turn right as if with military precision, and finally stop—just outside his door! By then, Terry was well beneath his covers with no plan to peek out any time soon. But the incident ended there, nothing more happened. It is one of Terry's scariest memories. He knew without a doubt that he was the only person home that night.

That may have been one of his most frightening memories, but the evil man with the red eyes was certainly no picnic either. Terry was having trouble staying asleep one night as he lay on the top bunk with his head tucked into the corner of the wall, because he kept having nightmares that "an evil man with red eyes, dressed all in black, said 'I am coming to get you.'" It went on several times a night for several nights in a row, so his mother finally suggested that he turn around and sleep with his head at the other end of the bed. Maybe the position or direction he was in was somehow causing the nightmares—a Feng Shui oversight, perhaps. Under the circumstances, anything was worth a try. The nightmares did stop with his head at the foot of his bed; but Terry could still feel the man with the red eyes there, waiting, "for what, I don't know." The evil man never did get Terry, as it had threatened; but he apparently got Janis.

She saw him, too. She remembers his red eyes peering through her window one night, and she tried desperately to find an explanation, hoping they were a reflection from something, but no source was to be found for the strange lights. They returned again and again, night after night—the two red lights that stayed perfectly aligned as they moved steadily across her room, never blinking. She watched as they moved from the window toward her closet, where she always felt a "heavy, foreboding presence." She sensed that whomever they belonged to was responsible for the heavy weight she felt on top of her in bed sometimes. Whatever it was, its breath on her face was hot—not at all the chilling air you'd expect from a ghost. This was one of the things her sister, Becky, had warned her about and that she couldn't believe until she experienced it herself. Then she understood all too well why her sister, Mary, slept with a Bible and even a knife—and why she was so eager to move out.

Unfortunately, Mary didn't fare much better when she did move. She rented an apartment on Arsenal Street in Watertown that she shared with at least three ghosts—not exactly her first choice for desirable roommates.

Mary had told her mother from day one that her apartment was haunted. Her brother, Terry, who was sixteen at the time, needed proof, so he was invited to spend the night. The first night proved uneventful. But the next time he stayed at his big sister's apartment was a night he'll never forget. Janis went along that time, as well. Mary had told them that one of the ghosts was in the kitchen and would make itself known by "the smell of rotting, decaying flesh." Before they left the apartment to get groceries for the sleepover, Terry helped his sister clean up. He said they used straight bleach so all they could smell when they left was a nice, squeaky clean apartment. Nothing else. About a half hour later, when they returned from the store, the door was wide open, even though it had been locked when they left, and "the stench of rotting flesh permeated the air." Minutes later the smell was gone.

That night at Mary's apartment, Terry had just fallen asleep when he heard Janis's "famous eardrum-shattering scream." Mary ran in to check on her, and just as she did, Terry said "a ghost came in and scratched my back very hard with both hands, then disappeared." He asked Mary what had happened, and she said Janis had been visited by the ghost of a little boy who had no eyes and who wanted to play with her.

There was another ghost, according to Mary, that stayed in the closet. She showed Terry the closet, and he said that when he walked in, he definitely felt a presence there. He had all the proof he needed that his sister's new apartment was truly haunted. Little did he know that he would buy his own home on Gifford Street a few years later that would also turn out to be haunted. But for the time being, he had his hands full with the ghosts at his family's home on the Sulphur Springs Road.

Back at that house, Janis had gone up to her room one night to get something and encountered an evil presence trying to chase her out. She didn't see it—there were no red or empty eyes boring into her this time —but she could feel it right down to her bones, and it was hot on her heels. She felt that it was the devil himself, and she panicked, racing down the stairs so fast that her brother and father came to her rescue. Her brother gave her his cross pendant for protection, and she still has it to this day. Her father prayed with her, and things seemed to improve for a couple of years.

The last notable incident Janis recalls happened in 1995. Her niece and nephew were visiting, and her niece was rooming with Janis, since she had the bunk beds. The girls often talked into the wee hours, and that was why they happened to be awake when a car pulled up to the house. They heard the car doors open and close, and they heard a man call

Janis's name and a different man call her niece's name. The voices were not familiar to them, and the girls had no boyfriends at the time to point the finger at. But most perplexing of all is the fact that there was no car when they looked out the window!

Just before dawn the next morning, Janis woke to find the bunk beds shaking violently. Her niece had also awakened and was leaning, terrified, over the side of the top bunk asking Janis what was making the bed shake. She begged Janis to make it stop, but there was nothing either could do. They could only wait for it to pass, which thankfully didn't take long.

Terry's last experience worth mentioning in that house happened in 1993. It was a balmy Friday evening, and his family had enjoyed a cookout under the stars, with the light from the back room casting a glow over the large backyard. Terry was sitting outside smoking a Doral and unwinding from a busy week, lost in no particular thought. That was when he saw something little and black scurry across the yard in the distance. Squinting and leaning forward a bit, he could see there were actually four of the little "creatures," and their eyes were red. They all seemed to find different objects to hide behind, and then they just stayed still, as if they were watching him. Terry could still feel the creatures with the red eyes there, waiting, "for what, I don't know..." A familiar feeling of dread washed over him.

Close Encounters With Orbs

Lake George

Rick Dalrymple has had several visitations by deceased loved ones since he was a child, so he knows what a spirit looks like. But one evening last summer, after a relaxing dinner cruise on Lake George, he saw something he'd never seen before. Ghost lights, presumably; better known as orbs.

It was about nine o'clock at night, and he was driving back to the nearby Roaring Brook Resort in Lake Luzerne where he was staying. The incident occurred as he was passing through an area about two miles south of Lake George on Route 9N, where there was nothing on either side of the highway except forest.

Rick said, "Suddenly a light that I would describe as being about the size of—and maybe a bit brighter than—a night-light came out of the forest on my right, crossed the road about ten feet above the car, and went into the forest on the other side. I knew right away that it couldn't have been a lightning bug. It was too big and bright. And I wasn't in an area where there were any electrical lines arcing or anything like that." He made sure of that when he returned to the scene the following morning to rule out other possible causes for what he'd seen.

Having come up with nothing else that could explain the incident, he said, "All I can think is that it was a 'ghost light' of some sort. I've been wondering if this is a common experience in the Lake George area. I saw two more of the strange lights the following night, near the same area. They weren't bright like the first one, but they were much bigger and crossed the road about eye level going from left to right."

Interestingly, almost all sightings of ghosts and spirits occur at eye level. It only adds more validation to the argument that Rick must have encountered genuine spirit orbs on the highway near Lake George, two nights in a row. I have to believe that someone else out there has, as well.

Don't Make Us Leave

Lacona

Residence of Robyn Sawyer and Fiance Tim Stevens, Lacona

Belle Salisbury walked into the attic of the pre-Civil War home she was investigating for her friend, Robyn Sawyer, in the town of Lacona. It was a typical old attic—dusty, dark, a bit cluttered, as one would expect. She paused to see if she "picked up" anything. She has the gift of "the second sight" and senses the spirit world, not only in sight, but in sound and feeling. She blurted out to nobody in particular, "I feel like someone is looking out this window and waiting." It was a large window overlooking the rear of the house, which is now an open meadow. Turning to her husband Gary, she asked him to take a photograph, as they typically do of each room during an investigation of a home believed to be haunted. With that, she gave the room one more cursory glance, turned, and walked out, leaving Gary alone in the attic while he unsuspectingly took what would become Belle's "prized photo."

When the digital photographs were downloaded on Belle's computer screen, the photograph taken in the attic showed a woman with a checked dress or cape over her shoulders standing to the left of the big window and looking out—the same window Belle had sensed someone was looking out that day. Even though everyone who was in on the investigation knew Gary had been alone in the attic when that photo was taken, they all still asked each other, incredulously, if there was any possible chance someone else was there. The image of the woman was so clear; surely it had to be someone real. But it wasn't. In fact, there is nothing checkered in the entire attic, nor is there anything that looked remotely like the garment the apparition was wearing. The photograph is a spirit photographer's dream.

Belle is a sought-out psychic with boundless energy and a heart of gold. For more than thirty years, she has deftly straddled the boundary where the physical world meets the spirit realm—with one foot firmly planted here, and one foot respectfully perched over there. In this way she is able to help those on this side receive information from those on the other side, including deceased loved ones, angels, and spirit guides. The natural extension of her abilities is to investigate haunted homes, communicate with the visiting spirits, and explain to the physical inhabitants of dwelling places why their property is being haunted.

One of those homes was the residence of Robyn and her fiancé, Tim Stevens, at 2041 County Route 48 in the town of Lacona. A number of incidents led Robyn to request a home investigation from Belle. The family was hearing footsteps and knocking within the walls, and they were seeing unexplainable—yet, undeniable—evidence of the presence of spirits in their home. They asked Belle for her assistance, not to determine *if* their house was haunted, but to help them understand *why* it was. There was no question in Robyn's mind that it was truly haunted, not after she saw an apparition of someone from the legs down wearing a

Photo by Gary Salisbury

Checked apparition in attic to left of window, Lacona

pair of old boots and black pants. Not after she watched the door of her dryer open unassisted by human hands, then close and start up again— all with nobody touching it. She often sees shadows out of the corner of her eye, as many people do in haunted homes.

Robyn's daughter, Paige, who is nine years old, hears voices coming from the attic, which is where Belle's husband snapped the picture of the female apparition. And she once asked her mother who the man was that was coming into the kitchen from the porch. Paige watched him come in, walk through the door, then turn around, and walk back out. She said the man was dressed in black. Although they were both looking out the same window at the same time, Robyn couldn't see him, so she simply told Paige it was one of those things that she's able to see that not everyone can. Other family members feel as if they are being watched while in the sitting room, which is located directly below the attic.

Robyn's seventeen-year-old son, Jeremy, admits to feeling like he's being watched whenever he goes to bed. Belle felt the presence of an older gentleman with either a stiff leg or a wooden leg while she was standing in Jeremy's room. She sensed that he was very protective of Jeremy.

One of the more remarkable incidents in the home occurred one night when Paige watched, enchanted, as the clothes from the clothing rack in her sister's room floated around the room on their hangers, *with nobody in the room*. Bewitching, to say the least.

A pentagram, a symbol of protection for those who feel the presence of 'others,' was etched into the wood behind a wall of plaster and lath. Because most homes prior to World War II were built with lath and plaster walls, as opposed to the drywall method more commonly used today, the symbol must have been put there many, many years ago. Furthermore, a previous owner informed Robyn that on the floorboard in the sitting room, they had discovered a cross burned into the wood. Portions of that flooring had been replaced prior to Robyn and her family moving in. Clearly, something unusual had occurred in the house long before the Sawyers ever moved in.

They know that their home was built prior to the Civil War and that a railroad company owned it in the past. They also know that their property was once the biggest farm in the area, and they were told that a man hanged himself in the old barn.

So what did Belle discover from her walk-through of the home? As mentioned earlier, she felt the presence of someone in the attic, even before a photograph offered proof of it. She said that the basement "felt like death," and the others who were investigating with her had similar feelings. Robyn agrees that the basement is the one place in the house that feels a bit uncomfortable to go into. Belle sensed a lot of spirits in the basement area, particularly in a filled-in hole in the cellar floor. She also felt there was another room *beneath* the basement floor, and when Tim did some digging after the investigation, he discovered a rather large open space was, indeed, beneath the basement floor. To date, they've not decided whether to investigate this 'secret' room further, for fear of opening something that might best be left to rest. Belle wonders if it was perhaps "a hiding place for those desiring not to be found during impromptu inspections," like one could expect during the days of the Underground Railroad movement.

A member of Belle's investigative team said he got the feeling that many people were crammed together in the tight and dark basement and wonders if it was slaves hiding out on their journey. Whatever the situation was at the house, the general consensus was that a lot of people were in the basement on a temporary basis, and there had quite possibly been death in that basement, due to living conditions at the time. Perhaps it was necessary to bury people beneath the floor, rather than having a proper burial, to prevent the discovery and interruption of whatever clandestine operations might have been going on there. Of course, that's pure speculation without further historical information.

One person we do know existed in the home's early days (and continues to dwell there now in spirit) is a man Belle spoke to when she saw him in the foyer. He was a nervous sort of individual wearing tattered clothes and jeans, and he was wringing a floppy cloth hat in his hands, saying to Belle, "Miss Ma'am, Miss Ma'am, please don't make us leave." Belle assured him that she wasn't there to make 'them' leave, to which the man nodded his head graciously and backed away. She said the way he stopped at the entrance to the kitchen led her to believe that he was forbidden to enter any room beyond the foyer, or sitting room. He might well have been hired help from long ago, but he isn't ready to leave this old home just yet; and who knows how many others he was speaking for.

The family doesn't mind sharing their home with the kindly caretaker or anyone else residing there in spirit. Robyn said they feel very safe and wouldn't give up their home for the world.

An Army of Ghosts

Watertown

Terry is intimately familiar with haunted houses. He grew up in one, his sister lived in one, and now Terry has a haunted home of his own. As far as he knows, he's the third owner of the house he bought in 1996 at 24200 Gifford Street, Route 12 South. It was built in 1940 with leftover lumber from Fort Drum construction.

From the moment he first entered the house, Terry suspected it was haunted. His sixth sense is well-developed, thanks to childhood experiences and to his ancestors. Terry's maternal grandmother was Native American and, as such, was very much attuned to the spirit world. He believes she passed her 'gift' on to him, as well as to his sisters and his nephew. Terry's strongest ability is clairvoyancy (clear vision). It allows him to "get a mental picture of ghosts" so that he can describe them and determine if they are dangerous or harmless.

The first incident on Gifford Street occurred in 1998, two years after he moved in. He set a tool on the table, and it promptly disappeared. Ghosts don't like changes to their familiar environments, so they desperately try to hinder any such efforts. It's almost comical how often tools come up missing in haunted homes that are under repair. Typically, these missing objects reappear either one or two days later, if they reappear at all. Terry's tool was returned to its rightful position two days later, precisely where he'd last seen it, which is more than he can say for his unopened Buick Skyhawk model kit that he had set on the washing machine and planned to build. Terry searched high and low, but the model kit has never been found.

Shortly after his first paranormal experience, Terry came home from work one day and walked into the living room to turn on the fan. He walked in on a spirit couple arguing about finances—a timeless dispute —right there in his living room! The woman said, "I don't know how we're going to pay for it." The man responded, but with something unintelligible. Terry got a strong mental image of the two and saw that they were elderly with white hair. The woman was wearing a modest, floral print dress, and her husband wore a spiffy white shirt, red suspenders, and gray pants. After that one incident, he never saw (or heard) the penny-pinching pair again.

Another time, he was in the kitchen when he heard a young woman say, "Terry?" Without thinking, he replied, "Yes?" But he received no further response and was unable to pick up a mental image of the woman. A year or two later, however, he was cleaning out the attic for the first time and discovered a mirror that apparently had a spirit attached to it. He saw a female with long, red hair who was wearing a white, flowing dress. She seemed to be asking him for something, but he didn't understand what. He believes she's the one who called to him in the kitchen that day.

In light of the events that were transpiring, Terry set out to learn more about the history of his home and to see if he could determine just how many ghosts he was dealing with. So he bought a dowsing rod—a forked stick that guides the user to hidden knowledge with the aid of supernatural forces. More commonly, it's used to find sources of underground water (water-witching), but it served Terry's purposes exceedingly well. There weren't just one or two ghosts in his residence. No— there were literally dozens, and that was before he visited a nearby cemetery and dragged home even more—albeit, unintentionally. It was like a whole army of ghosts. (Maybe they came with the lumber from Fort Drum!)

Terry doesn't know who all of the ghosts are, but he did figure out who one of them is. He believes it's the spirit of his mother. About a year after her passing, on a Saturday afternoon in broad daylight, he heard her call his name. The familiar voice was followed immediately by that of the young female ghost who had previously called his name. Simultaneously, he smelled his mother's rose-scented perfume. The same evening, Terry was talking to someone online who asked him if he'd ever been touched by a ghost. Just as he was about to respond that he hadn't, he felt "a single, ice-cold finger on his bare right forearm." It was a shocking moment, even for a guy who thought he'd seen, heard, or felt just about everything.

About a week later, he was chatting online when his parents' wedding picture fell a good six feet from the top of his CD player. The only explanation was that someone wanted to get Terry's attention. It's likely that it was his mother, since she is deceased and, thus, was in the best position to pull such a stunt.

At the suggestion of a friend, Terry tried his hand at taking electronic voice phenomenon recordings (EVP)—capturing on cassette the sounds of ghosts and spirits that are not otherwise perceived by the human ear. He used a standard tape player and waited patiently in his silent house. His efforts paid off. Sounds were caught on the tape that had no business being there. Nobody was with him when he made the first recording; yet, he picked up the sounds of music, papers rustling, pans clanging in the kitchen, something banging around upstairs, strange footsteps, and some incoherent murmuring. Terry's suspicions were confirmed, and he has it on tape.

Another week passed and he saw a real spirit—not just the mental image of one, the way he usually saw them. This time he actually saw one with the naked eye. He said he was walking by the couch and discovered that he had some uninvited company of the supernatural kind. The ghost was light gray and had no discernible human shape. It passed about five or six inches in front of him, and just as he started to say, "What the…," it disappeared. Unfortunately, it would be back.

The aforementioned ghost returned in December 2002. Terry was asleep at 1:30 A.M. when his sixth sense kicked in. He opened his eyes just in time to see the gray ghost floating into his room. It boldly came straight over to him and bore down on his chest and on one of his arms. He felt certain it was trying to smother him but finally managed to break free from the ghost's grip using his free arm for leverage. Several nights later, the same thing happened at exactly the same time, 1:30 A.M., but this time it used even more force to hold Terry. It had both of his arms pinned down, apparently remembering Terry's previous escape. When it got to the point that Terry couldn't move and could barely even breathe, he got mad. Real mad. *The nerve of this...this THING!* Terry hadn't done anything to upset it that he knew of. He'd actually asked it nicely to get off him and leave him alone. How dare it do this to him in his own home! With his options quickly fading, Terry realized the only weapon at his immediate disposal was his mind. He mustered all of the mental strength he could and gave the menacing gray blob a huge mental shove—with a few choice words for added emphasis. It was certainly a unique example of mind over matter (or mind over *something*). The entity hasn't been seen or felt since.

Not all of Terry's encounters with ghosts have been negative. He credits a ghost he now recognizes as "John" with actually saving his life one day. Last summer he was sound asleep when he heard someone yell, "Hey!" His eyes popped open, and he realized he was feeling very drained and decided he'd better check his blood sugar. As a diabetic, he has to be diligent in keeping his blood sugar levels normal. His had dropped to a dangerously low level when the ghost shouted at him. If he hadn't been awakened right then, he may have died.

Photo by Terry

Orb on left side of stairwell that Terry believes is John, Watertown

John may be a do-gooder, but another ghost prefers mischief. Terry recently took one of his younger sisters grocery shopping. Because of his medical condition, he has to buy and eat certain foods. So, besides the usual items one gets when grocery shopping, he also made sure to pick up a three-pound bag of tangerines and two pounds of sliced turkey breast. Terry dropped his sister off at her house and stayed to visit for a couple hours, then headed home to put his own groceries away. A couple of days later, he went to grab a tangerine, but they were gone. He asked Becky if she might have mistaken his groceries for hers, even though he knew she hadn't. She replied as expected. It was a mystery, but Terry figured he had enough other things to get by until he got back to the grocery store again.

But then the same thing happened again. He bought groceries, put them away, then went to the fridge to get some turkey, and the turkey breast was missing. He told the hungry ghost to return his food. He tried everything—asking nicely, asking angrily, begging and pleading—it was like dealing with a tired toddler. Finally, he said he didn't appreciate the practical joke and that it was stealing, plain and simple (not to mention dangerous, because of his diabetic condition). While those particular groceries never resurfaced, he must have said something right, because the next time he got groceries, nobody messed with them.

Maybe there's hope yet for the large army of ghosts and their unwitting sergeant.

The home on Gifford Street is Private Property—Please Do Not Disturb

Happily Ever After

Madrid

There's an old house in Madrid on a road less traveled that looks like a classic haunted house. We all know looks can be deceiving, but according to a family who lived there years ago, what you see with this place is what you get. And they got more than just an eyeful!

Everything started out fine, like the calm before the storm. Joyce, her husband, and their seven children moved into the place and immediately set to work adding personal touches to make it feel more like home. They were all content in their house in the country, and before long they'd gotten into an evening routine that included popcorn and a movie before bed—simple pleasures of life in these parts.

One evening Joyce was sitting in the living room with her children when she noticed what looked like car lights coming down the road toward their house. It was odd, because they rarely had visitors on their remote stretch of road, especially at that time of night. She stared at the lights curiously but was taken aback when she saw that they were approaching her yard at lightning speed and were heading straight toward their house—and they weren't slowing down! Before she could gather her wits, the light, (it now looked like a huge, single ball of light suspended in mid-air) was upon her. It hovered in front of the bay window of the living room, shining with such intensity that it filled the entire room with blinding light. Joyce and the children stared in disbelief, and then, in a split second, the ball of light vanished before their eyes. The stunned family quickly dispersed around the house, turning on every light, to alleviate their fear. It was a strange, sleepless night.

Eventually, the living room incident was pushed to the back of their minds, and life went on, but the old house never again felt as comfortable as it did when they first moved in. In fact, the longer they stayed, the less hospitable it became. It's not that it felt overtly hostile to any of them; it's just that they felt almost as if they were sharing the property with someone else—someone who seemed annoyed at their presence.

Joyce's daughter, Nat, shared a "dark and gloomy" room with one of her sisters. She always reached around the corner of the doorway to turn on the light before daring to step in, because she couldn't shake the feeling that someone or something was lurking just inside the door. Her sixth sense was well-tuned, it turned out. Not long after the family was accosted by the ball of light in the living room, Nat woke one night to the sight of a woman standing in her bedroom. She was enveloped in a golden glow and wore a gown that seemed to be flowing in the wind. Nat assumed the woman was a ghost and yanked the covers up over her head, telling herself to count to three—*one, two, two and a half, three….* When she peeked back out from under the blankets, the mysterious "golden woman" had disappeared. Today, Nat believes the woman may have been an angel, rather than a ghost.

A week or so later, Nat was awakened by a hand touching her face. She refused to open her eyes, because she realized she hadn't heard anyone come into the room—no footsteps across the squeaky floorboards—which meant that it couldn't have been her parents or siblings. And nobody she knew could float silently through the air. Believing that the golden woman had returned, and still assuming she was a ghost, she was "frozen with fear." After what seemed like an eternity, the hand finally lifted from her face. Her sister, asleep in the bed beside her, later admitted that she, too, occasionally felt someone sit on her bed in the middle of the night, even though she never saw anyone actually there. And her brother admitted that he once saw a man wearing a top hat in his room.

One of the other children had a bedroom adjacent to the attic. The attic door was accessible from her bedroom, so she could open the door and walk right in. She told her family that there was always noise coming from the attic, like someone was moving stuff around. Built in the mid-eighteen hundreds, the house had an attic full of antiques, but there was never anyone in the attic when the noises were heard. And nobody ever answered when the girl asked who was there. Every so often, the metal hinge that held the attic door on shook and jiggled, like someone was trying to get out—or *in*!

Eventually, the entire family had reached the same conclusion…they were not alone, and they were not welcomed in their own home. But this story has a happy ending. You see, the family was eager to move out, and the ghosts were glad to see them go. And they all lived (or haunted) happily ever after.

Harriet, Harriet, Harriet

Lisbon

Jennifer is not sure why she opened her eyes that night and looked toward her bedroom door, but when she did, she realized she had company. *Uninvited company*. The bearded man was staring solemnly at her, not moving or reacting to her awakening in any way. At first glance, she thought it was one of her Amish neighbors, because he was dressed in plain nineteenth-century clothing. She thought he must have needed something, so he showed himself in. If she had been more awake, she would have been offended by such a rude intrusion, but her mind was too busy processing the details of the apparition's appearance to question its presence. He wore wool pants and a wool coat with brass buttons down the front. The buttons were very vivid. He was "a little fuzzy around the edges," but she couldn't see through him or anything. She had no reason to believe he *wasn't* a solid human being. He even spoke to her, but she forgot his words moments later, just as he vanished before her eyes. She promptly jumped out of bed to make sure her children and nieces were safe, and then she remembered something. The Amish don't wear buttons.

The man who appeared in her doorway could have been anyone, but he definitely wasn't anyone who was alive at the time of the incident described above. In fact, he had probably been dead for many, many years. The historic house on State Route 68 in the Town of Lisbon is just shy of two hundred years old. It was originally built as a tavern, so the man Jennifer saw that night may well have been a tavern patron from long ago—he certainly looked the part. In fact, he may have been the

27

individual who was thought to have fallen down the stairs of the tavern —perhaps in a drunken stupor—many, many years ago.

It certainly seems plausible that someone fell down the stairs at one time, because the sickening thud of a body bouncing down the steps was heard several years ago by six people at the very same time. Jennifer's family and their two guests were awakened one night to the unmistakable sound of an actual body falling down the grand staircase in the middle of their home. They all raced out of their rooms expecting to see someone lying battered and broken at the bottom of the stairs, but nobody—*no body*—was there.

Strangely enough, a descendant of the original builder named Jennifer as an heir in his will, and she had only met him once. Either she made a remarkable first impression on the man, or fate had a hand in the matter. She and her husband have lived in the house they seemed destined to own for more than twenty-seven years now, and they have experienced countless unexplainable incidents during that time. Some are more trivial than others, like tapping sounds on the windows, mysterious cold spots throughout the house, and visitors to the home asking pointedly if the house is haunted, just because it feels like it is. Every member of the family has had something paranormal occur to them. But the majority of the more significant incidents have involved only Jennifer.

For example, an expensive painting has fallen off the wall three times—once in what appeared to be slow motion right before Jennifer's eyes. Each time it happened, the nail remained firmly embedded in the plaster, and the wire on the back of the painting stayed intact. Considering that the nail was angled slightly upward to ensure that the painting would never slide off, it's impossible to fathom how it got off the wall and onto the floor at all, especially in one piece. The mechanics of such an action would require someone to deliberately lift the painting up before pulling it away from the wall; yet, in each case, nobody was near it.

Another incident that was almost too coincidental, if not paranormal, was when Jennifer and her husband chose the location in their yard to construct a large woodshed. Unknowingly, they began construction on the exact site of a former carriage house. Amazingly, the measurements for their building were identical to those of the carriage house —

a structure they hadn't even known about at the time and whose foundation was entirely concealed by earth when they broke ground.

Jennifer learned some of the history of her house in a mysteriously orchestrated way. She answered the door one day to find an elderly woman, unknown to her, who had parked her car right smack in the center of the highway out front—it was an accident waiting to happen. Or so it seemed, until fate reared its clever head again. Jennifer followed the endearingly feeble-minded visitor back out to her car—more to make sure she moved it off the highway than anything—and was astonished to see a book of memoirs on the seat of the car that had been written by the son-in-law of the builder of her very own home. The old woman kindly presented the wonderful book to Jennifer.

Jennifer has heard a woman's voice several times, and a crying baby or child is often heard throughout the house. The woman said things and relayed messages that, while clear at the time of the occurrences, were forgotten as soon as her voice trailed off. Three people heard the voice at the same time on one occasion; yet, incredibly, none could recall what was said afterward. Jennifer explained that when these ghostly voices are heard, it feels as if you are in a "trance-like or dream-like state," even though you are wide awake and it's daytime. She described it as a surreal experience that leaves you with complete amnesia regarding what was said to you, even though you recall that the message was coherent at the time of the incident.

Whom could the voices belong to? The author of the memoirs left a few possible clues in his writings. Harriet, the daughter of the builder and wife of the author of the memoirs, lived there and served as tavern keeper with her husband George until she went insane during the Civil War era. After attempting to drown herself in the basement cistern of Jennifer's home, she was taken away to an insane asylum in Utica, leaving behind George and their five-year-old adopted daughter, both whom she never saw again. Until someone can offer a better explanation,

Jennifer believes the woman and the young child she senses in her home are actually Harriet and Harriet's adopted daughter.

Harriet supposedly died at the age of fifty, but George didn't receive word of her passing until weeks later, because means of communication were very slow back then. Immediately upon notification, he had the asylum send her casket to him by train, and when it arrived, he dutiful-ly buried her and placed a stone marker near her grave. Several weeks after the burial, a friend who was unaware of her passing visited the asy-lum in Utica and asked how she was doing. He was told she was upstairs recovering! When he told George, the grieving man didn't know who was buried in nearby Campbell's Cemetery. Not knowing which death date was the correct one, he placed different stones over her grave, each with a different date of death. At the time that he wrote his memoirs when he was in his nineties, George apparently still didn't know if he had buried the right person in the cemetery or when his beloved wife had actually died, and he never had the heart (or the stomach) to open the casket to confirm the identity of the corpse.

Maybe Harriet, too, is still confused about whether or not she died, because she continues to make her presence known in many ways to Jennifer. She appears often to her, but only as a very vague apparition—not nearly as solid as the man she saw in her bedroom doorway that she mistook for an Amish neighbor. But the most memorable thing about Harriet is her voice. Even though her words are never recalled, she speaks them very distinctly.

Jennifer believes Harriet is the type of ghost known as a poltergeist. She said, "My study of poltergeists confirmed that these 'ghosts' are friendly, have been well-documented, and are spirits of people who do not, or cannot, leave a certain locale. They most often exhibit them-selves in the presence of pre-pubescent children, which our daughters were during the most active time period. It was further revealed that if poltergeists approve of you, they will cease their activity, or, at worst, display themselves during times of disruption. Poltergeists like things to continue unchanged. (Indeed, the dismantling of their barn increased the activity.) They do not like to have furniture rearranged, and, ironically, neither do I. Documentation of their activity in other situations often includes returning furniture to its original positions."

In the summer of 1995, while her husband was helping his father install electric heaters in the newly-renovated attic space, a pair of elec-trician's pliers and sidecutters disappeared. They had been used just moments before, but to this day, they've never been found. At the same time, a wooden 3-D puzzle shaped like a ball disappeared from the same area. *The puzzle of the missing puzzle.* It, too, has never been recovered. Jennifer, her husband, and her mother- and father-in-law were all in the attic when the items vanished. Her father-in-law's first inclination was that one of the others present—possibly Jennifer's husband—had taken the objects as a prank, but none of them had come or gone during the time the incident took place. Jennifer's in-laws were left with no choice but to concede that the home was haunted, as Jennifer had told them.

Incidentally, during renovation of the attic, repeated knocking from the exterior of the knee-walls in that room was often heard. Just as Jennifer said, ghosts don't like to have their familiar surroundings altered in any way. If it is Harriet haunting the home, she certainly fits the profile of a poltergeist to a tee.

Also in the summer of 1996, a spring-operated wind-up music box that Jennifer's husband had made for one of their daughters, who is now grown, began to play for no apparent reason. The sentimental object sits on a shelf in the girl's old bedroom and hadn't been played in years. When she heard it, Jennifer went upstairs to investigate and found that the music box was playing its song, "Raindrops Keep Fallin' on My Head."

A few years ago, a kitchen drawer began to smoke from inside. Jennifer doused the smoke with water, but it still left a char mark in the drawer. She said, "A week before that, my husband turned the kitchen door into a Dutch door, and I began to smell an odor of garbage. When I smelled the char mark in the drawer, it was the same odor!" It made her wonder if it was some type of spontaneous combustion, or if Harriet was simply bent out of shape about "her" door being changed. Whatever the reason for the drawer smoldering, Jennifer admits it was a bit drastic, even for the typically mischievous Harriet. "This was no minor prank, in my opinion," she said.

Though some of the paranormal incidents that have taken place in the home have been frightening, for the most part, Jennifer and her family are not overly concerned. They certainly have no plans to leave their wonderful home. Even though Jennifer would never seek out such activity, she admits that some of the incidents have actually been rather interesting and pleasant, only adding more charm and character to the old place. She believes that not everybody has the ability to notice the spirit realm but said, "I am honored to have been chosen."

John Hoover Inn

Evans Mills

Photo by Author

John Hoover Inn, Evans Mills

The John Hoover Inn, on the corner of Main and Noble Streets in Evans Mills, was built more than 175 years ago by its namesake, John Hoover, a former captain stationed in Sackets Harbor during the War of 1812. Over the past two centuries, the inn has certainly seen a lot of satisfied customers come and go. For the most part, bar patrons heed last call and depart shortly thereafter; but every once in awhile, long after the bar closes for the night, a rather boisterous crowd can be heard hooting and hollering into the wee hours of the morning! Heard, but not seen. This crowd is an elusive lot. The rumors may well be true—the John Hoover Inn really *is* haunted.

John Hoover built and opened the brick hotel in 1827. Many tavern-keepers have owned and operated the inn since Captain Hoover's tenure, but that honor is currently held by Stephanie Comini. The ambitious mother of three and wife of a Fort Drum army sergeant took hold of the reigns on November 1, 2002. Under her management, the inn is open daily as a bar, a lodging place, and even a tanning center. Six rooms are rented by the week, and part of the upstairs is leased by A Step Above hair studio.

Stephanie said that it's the upstairs tenants who have heard people coming and going on the floor beneath them—right where the bar area is—long after closing time, even though the doors are always locked until morning. One night in October 2003, Stephanie was applying the final coat of a sealer to the new dance floor. She was well aware of the late hour, because she had set the clocks back that night for daylight savings. The next day, one of the occupants of a room upstairs asked her what time she finished the night before, because he had heard several people having a "good old time, laughing and clanging bottles" in the dining room at about 5:30 A.M. Stephanie had been alone doing the floor and had been gone a full two hours by the time the tenant heard the strange clattering downstairs; so she couldn't be to blame.

Another tenant heard the same thing that morning, so she walked downstairs to check out the noise; but it stopped. Then, just as she got back up the stairs, the same eerie disturbance began again. Determined to catch a glimpse of the merrymakers, she returned downstairs several times. Yet each time, the noise stopped and started again as soon as she made her way back up to her room. There were no signs of intruders or leftover bar patrons, and nothing was out of place. The new dance floor, still tacky with polyurethane, showed no evidence of usage. Clearly, nobody had walked or danced across it yet—floated, maybe—but certainly not *waltzed*.

The same night, one of the other tenants heard Victrola-type music coming from the beauty salon, but as he walked toward the door, the music stopped. Of course, when he walked away from the room, the music started again. According to Stephanie, the beautician has had clients come in with their children and grandchildren, and the children claim to talk to the ghost of a "lady in the hall" who tells them to 'shhh' and waves at them. So if you're looking for a hair-raising experience, A Step Above hair studio might be just the salon for you!

Other people have noticed a strong sensation of being watched from behind when they are in the basement, even though no one is there. Lights are known to inexplicably turn on and off in the dining room. It's no wonder some regulars claim the old building is "full of ghosts." In a building as old as the John Hoover Inn—and with such a rich history—people are bound to wonder if it's haunted.

A popular and enduring tale involving the inn is that the ghost of Ameriga Vespucci, a descendant of the famed explorer Amerigo Vespucci, haunts the building. She passed through the area with two prominent men in 1841. As the story goes, their coach had stopped at the inn for the evening, and one of the men (President Martin Van Buren's son, John) wagered the weary damsel in a game of cards with the other man, George Parish—a wealthy businessman from Ogdensburg. Van Buren lost, and the lovely Ameriga left the inn arm-in-arm with Mr. Parish. Although there is no way to confirm or deny the identity of the inn's current "nighttime guests," a compelling argument can be made on behalf of Ms. Vespucci's party and its lingering presence.

Come to think of it, Ms. Vespucci is also the subject of another North Country ghost legend. There's a widespread rumor that her spirit was once seen at the Remington Art Museum in Ogdensburg, though the museum staff denies it. If it were true, however, we could speculate that Ms. Vespucci, who died in Paris 138 years ago, continues to return to her old haunts along with the company she once kept.

Whatever the case may actually be, Stephanie Comini isn't saying the John Hoover Inn is haunted…or that it's not! What she is saying is that there are some pretty strange things that go on in the night, and she's not just referring to the antics of her, shall we say, more *lively* regulars. "As long as business is good, I'm not going to lose any sleep over it." She'll leave that to the tenants!

Meron's Restaurant

Plattsburgh

Meron's Bar & Restaurant, Plattsburgh

Grace Bergman and her mother live above Meron's Bar and Restaurant on the corner of Beekman and Bailey. This allows Grace, the owner/operator, to keep an eye on the business that has been in her family since Prohibition in 1931; and it allows her mother to keep tabs on old "Uncle Maynard," her brother who passed away in 1984, after living and working at the bar for fifty-three years. He must be even fonder of the family business than he is of Heaven, because he keeps coming

37

back—which is a pretty high compliment to pay to Meron's!

Grace and her mother believe that Maynard is the only one haunting them. In fact, they're absolutely certain it's him. His usual morning ritual for much of his adult life had been to go downstairs to the bar and have his coffee, bacon, and cinnamon rolls. The same exact smells keep emerging over and over—fourteen years after he passed on—even though the bar doesn't even serve bacon and cinnamon rolls. And, they got rid of the coffee pot after Maynard died, because he was the only one who drank it! Nevertheless, those particular mouth-watering odors continue to permeate the air, usually after closing time. Grace said, "The smells are very strong and very frequent, but they are not at all scary."

If not for the familiar scents that incriminate Maynard, it would be difficult to identify who the bar's spirit visitor is, because the only other 'ghostly' things that happen are very typical and even a bit humdrum (no offense, Maynard). The television set comes on by itself when nobody is in the room. Grace and her mother often hear someone going into the cellar when Meron's is closed. They assume it's Maynard "just going about his business." Likewise, unexplained footsteps are often heard overhead by employees in the basement fetching more bottles of liquor.

Employees have also seen bottles and glasses fall unassisted from shelves; and at least one bartender, Laura Whalen, feels as if someone is standing behind her when she's in the basement, but she's quick to add that it doesn't feel malevolent. Everyone knows it's just Maynard— watching over the family business from the "Other Side."

Nightmare on Elm Street

Plattsburgh

Photo by Author

Apartment house at 44 Elm Street, Plattsburgh

One of the tenants at 44 Elm Street experienced a doozy of an encounter with the unknown that left him sleeping with a knife under his pillow for weeks. He'd always seen shadows out of the corner of his eye while living there—always in the same area, too—but nothing that was more than he could handle. Then the tall, dark stranger appeared in his room, wielding a knife, and the fear it instilled will haunt him always. It was a real-life nightmare on Elm Street, but he wasn't dreaming.

He thought the form silhouetted in the moonlight in front of his bedroom window was his landlord, Connie Repas, because she was the only person with access to his locked apartment. By the time he realized it wasn't her, he was fully awake and terrified. He was face-to-face with an unknown intruder who he was certain was going to harm him. He didn't see the knife, but he strongly sensed that the prowler was brandishing one. He felt that his life was in danger, and he knew the menacing figure had the upper hand in the matter. He decided he had only two choices —lie there, watching and waiting; or jump up from the bed and confront the guy. He chose to lie and wait.

For what seemed like six to ten minutes, he lie motionless, knowing that he was being watched. The stalker could smell his fear, he knew it. But the tenant remained outwardly calm, trying to show no reaction whatsoever, and soon the dark form slipped across the room to an archway and up two stairs, vanishing through the sealed-off door that would lead to one of the other tenant's spare bedrooms. That spare room in the upstairs apartment has seen more paranormal activity than any other room in the house.

Aside from the occasional paranormal incident, the house that Connie inherited when her mother passed away is actually quite comfortable and peaceful. There are four apartments—two upstairs and two down. The house was built in 1895 and has been in Connie's family since 1957. Nobody has died there since her family bought it, but, she said, "Prior to that is anyone's guess." Connie lives downstairs now, but has lived in one of the upstairs apartments as well. A few unforgettable encounters took place in that upstairs apartment, now occupied by Laura and John Whalen.

First, in 1978 when she was out of town, Connie's roommate was asleep in the spare bedroom (the one with the most paranormal activity), when he awoke to a smoke-filled room. Thinking that the house was on fire, he frantically searched for the source of the smoke, even though he couldn't smell any. In fact, it didn't smell like anything, but there was a very visible smoke or haze of some sort. He raced downstairs and woke Connie's mother up, and when they realized the so-called 'smoke' couldn't be explained, the man refused to go back up to his apartment to sleep. In fact, he never slept there again, unless Connie was home. Connie's mother, described as "the most honest person on earth," didn't tell her daughter about the incident until years later, because she didn't want her to "get all dramatic about it."

The next time something happened was when Connie was in that same spare room. One night in 1980 or 1981, she woke to find "a tall, dark, shrouded figure" with no visible face looking down at her from the foot of her bed. Even through the darkness, she could tell by the ominous figure's outline that it was hooded and cloaked. She immediately felt that it was evil and—much like the tenant mentioned at the beginning of this story—she knew that if she showed her fear, it would only gain more power over her. So she turned to religion and started reciting "The Apostles Creed" out loud. She had been sitting up but leaned back on her pillow when she was sure she was winning the mental battle being waged with her. All the while, she continued reciting the prayer. Before long, the figure simply vanished—back into the shadows from whence it came.

Also like her upstairs tenant, Connie has seen "the shadowpeople"— shadows of entities that are in a different category altogether than ghosts. They are most often perceived in our peripheral vision and are now recognized as a common phenomenon in the paranormal field. But she pays little attention to them; they don't feel threatening and are just a familiar part of her existence. As long as they're not the ones responsible for dishes falling in the kitchen when nobody is in there, she doesn't mind their elusive presence.

Connie experienced another strange happening just recently. Sitting on an old wooden radio next to the window in her dining room is a framed picture of Weezer, her loveable Jack Russell terrier. It faces into the room, so people can see it as they pass through the house. Three times in a two-week period, she found the picture turned completely around, facing out the window. The dust beneath it—not that there's a lot of it, mind you—was undisturbed, so someone had to have physically picked it up, turned it around, and set it back down, ever so gingerly. For about three months straight, Connie was the only person in her apartment, literally; and she knows she didn't touch it.

Connie's friend and tenant, Laura Whalen, now lives with her husband John in the second-floor apartment that has the notorious "spare room." The room is painted antique pink and was nicely decorated when they rented the apartment, but the newlyweds use it for storage only. Laura said she doesn't know why, but she's in no hurry to furnish it as an extra bedroom—there's just something a little uncomfortable about it. She had no knowledge of anyone's experiences in that room before showing it to me, but she and John have both had experiences throughout the rest of their apartment.

They moved to 44 Elm Street in 2000. At first, they just dealt with silly, simple things like objects disappearing—mainly, John's Yankee baseball caps! If they turned up again, it was in obvious places right out in the open where they couldn't have been missed. But some of the caps never did turn up. And Laura lost a credit card one day. She searched high and low for it, in obvious and unlikely places, but she couldn't find it. Finally (since she was used to someone stealing her husband's ball caps already), she blurted out, "Give me back my credit card—I need it!" Shortly thereafter, it turned up right on the table, in too obvious a place for it to have been overlooked.

John once felt someone sit at the foot of their bed when Laura was asleep on the couch. His first thought was that it was "Bear," their large Black Lab, because sometimes the dog put his front paws up on the bed. But Bear was nowhere in sight. His next thought was that Laura had woken up and come in, but she hadn't. He got up and checked, and she was still fast asleep on the couch. Another time, John remembers turning off all of the lights and the television set before going to bed, just as he always does, but he woke in the middle of the night to find the TV turned back on. Bear may be a clever boy, but he's not *that* clever!

Speaking of Bear, he's had quite a few paranormal encounters of his own that he wasn't too happy about it. Forget the name—he's more like a *teddy* bear than a grizzly, but he does protect his territory and his masters, even under sometimes trying circumstances. He has a habit of going wherever he feels apprehension and standing there, as if he's trying to communicate to Laura and John that there's someone or something there that shouldn't be. One time, for example, Laura found him standing guard at the bathroom door, blocking the way for anyone to get in or out. Then, for no reason at all, he turned and went into the dining room and stood— obviously still agitated—looking at something only he could see.

Another incident took place just outside of the house. John brought Bear out, and they were standing under a tree. Just then, John felt a cold chill go through him, and at the same time, Bear began "freaking out" and acting viciously, which is entirely against his nature. He was looking up into the tree and looked like he was about to lunge. Luckily, he calmed down when John pulled him away from the tree and headed back inside. If it hadn't been for John feeling the cold chill, he might have thought Bear was about to turn on *him*, but both he and Bear were becoming accustomed to supernatural disturbances.

Bear has fended off phantoms at other places, as well. When Laura lived alone in a two-bedroom condominium on Margaret Street, Laura and Bear had their most terrifying encounter of all. Laura was suffering from writer's block when she was trying to write a paper (she was working on her Master's), so she decided to use an old Native American trick of burning sage to clear the atmosphere of anything malevolent. Being half Mohawk, she thought having the atmosphere cleared might help clear her mind so she could concentrate better. She went through the apartment, holding a smudge stick and smudged—or smoked—all of the corners of each room, as she'd been taught. *But she neglected to open any windows*, like she'd also been taught, so that whatever might have been in the atmosphere could escape. Her reasoning may have had something to do with the fact that burning sage can smell like marijuana (she'd heard), and she didn't want to take any chances that someone would misinterpret their olfactory impressions!

At any rate, shortly after her smudging routine, she came out of the bathroom and found Bear standing on alert in the hallway looking into the spare room. He was so determined to protect her and keep her from going in there that he actually backed up and sat on her feet, never taking his eyes off the room. Even so, Laura knew she had to check the room out, so she held Bear's collar and entered the room. Bear—who is a *huge dog*—was looking up and instantly assumed a submissive posture, as if he was terribly frightened. Laura opened the windows in the room, and the atmosphere lifted considerably. Whatever was there had apparently gone.

Back at the apartment on Elm Street, the most recent incident involved a friend of Laura's who was staying with them during

Christmastime last year. John and Laura slept on the couch so Laura's friend could have their bed. The next morning, the woman came out of the bedroom and said she'd had "a really strange experience in the bedroom." Apparently, she was looking out the window and thought Bear's tail was wagging against the curtain, because the curtain kept moving back and forth. Then she looked and realized it wasn't Bear. He wasn't around. The curtains continued to move even as she checked the window for a draft. But there was none. There was simply no explanation at all for the movement.

Most of the time, things are quiet and normal there—it's a lovely apartment house in a pleasant neighborhood. But every once in a while someone has a real-life "nightmare on Elm Street" when a looming Darth Vader-type makes their presence known in a most unpleasant way.

One Last Visit

Chamberlain Corners

Years ago, when Lois Caskinett was about ten or twelve years old, her aunt lived in the old school house at Chamberlain Corners. Lois and her cousin often went to visit the elderly Mrs. Chamberlain who lived next door. The woman, who Lois described as "a beautiful person," always enjoyed sitting and talking to the girls and showing them around her historic home, which was said to be part of the Underground Railroad. Unfortunately, Mrs. Chamberlain passed away before she ever got the chance to show the girls the secret passageways by the river that she had told them about.

Lois wasn't aware Mrs. Chamberlain had died, so one day when her parents drove out to Chamberlain Corners to visit Lois's aunt, the young girl eagerly jumped out of the car and headed straight over to Mrs. Chamberlain's house, as she always did. Just then she looked up to see the old woman—Mrs. Chamberlain herself—in one of the upstairs windows on the far right side of her house. Lois waved at her and called up that she was on her way over to visit. But Lois's aunt stopped her in her tracks and asked her where she was going. Lois told her to see Mrs. Chamberlain, of course. But she couldn't, her aunt told her, because Mrs. Chamberlain had passed away two weeks before. Lois shook her head, saying Mrs. Chamberlain couldn't be dead, because she had just seen her and waved at her. Her aunt would have none of it. Mrs. Chamberlain was gone, and that was that. Unconvinced, Lois turned and pointed back toward Mrs. Chamberlain's house defiantly to show her aunt that Mrs. Chamberlain was too alive—she was right there in the window. But to her chagrin, the old woman had vanished, never to be seen again.

Once Lois accepted the cold, hard fact that Mrs. Chamberlain really was gone, she decided that her elderly friend must have stayed around just long enough for Lois to pay her one last visit—just long enough to wave goodbye.

Tall, Dark & Dusty

Watertown

Teresa Bender had all she could do to understand what her daughter was saying into the phone. Morgan was watching TV when Teresa left for the library early that Saturday afternoon and nodded when her mother told her she'd call before she headed back home. Now, Teresa's stomach hit the floor as she listened to her daughter crying hysterically into the phone...something about seeing a man in the house who disappeared, so she was outside on the porch waiting for her mother to get home! *Good God!* The panic was tangible on both ends of the telephone line when Teresa hung up the phone and rushed home.

When she arrived, she found Morgan waiting anxiously on the porch, cradling the cordless phone as if it were her lifeline. Teresa managed to calm the teenager down enough so that she could tell her what happened. Morgan explained that she was lying on the living room floor next to the couch, watching TV, when she saw movement in the dining room out of the corner of her eye. She turned her head to look and saw "a tall, dark, young man walking towards the half wall next to the kitchen." There was a man in the house, a real, live man. He was wearing old clothes, and she said it looked like the "air around him and his clothes and skin was all dark and kind of dusty." The man didn't even see her, she said. "He just kept on walking toward the kitchen area and finally faded." Morgan managed to grab the phone and run out of the house.

Of all of the strange things that had happened in their house on Stone Street—and there had been many—that particular incident hit Teresa the hardest, seeing her oldest child so upset about something her own mother couldn't fix. Mothers are supposed to be able to fix anything. But no amount of comforting or cajoling could take away the memory of the man in black that was lodged in Morgan's mind. The girl was "absolutely petrified" and wouldn't sleep alone for weeks after her terrifying ordeal. Teresa knew she had no choice but to move, or find a way to rid her house of its apparent spirits.

The Benders moved from Clayton to their apartment house in Watertown in 1997. They hadn't been there long when they started to notice peculiar little things that didn't make sense. Teresa brushed the initial incidents off, figuring everyone was just spooked because it was a new place and an obviously very old building. Overworked imaginations, she thought, or the kids trying to trick her so they could keep the lights on all night—at least until they were used to their new surroundings. Besides, every old house has its creaking, snapping, and clanging sounds, right? Maybe if they ignored it long enough, it would go away; or they would just get used to it. But then things began to happen that couldn't be ignored.

The children's bedrooms were all upstairs, as was a tiny apartment that was occupied by another tenant in the building. Teresa's bedroom and the other main rooms were downstairs. The children complained of seeing dark, shadowy figures darting silently across their bedrooms at night. Teresa had no reason to doubt them. After all, she had seen something similar in the living room. She described it as "large and black and moving fast across the room—so fast, in fact, that I doubted what I actually saw." At least one of those times, the children had seen it at the same time she did.

Occasionally, when the whole family was downstairs, they heard heavy footsteps and the sound of objects being moved around in the upstairs hall and bedrooms, even though they knew nobody was up there. There were times when Teresa heard someone coming down the stairs late at night, and went out into the hallway to see who was out of bed; but nobody was there. In fact, once she was so sure of what she'd heard that she went upstairs to see who was up. The girls, Michelle and Morgan, told her they heard someone walking, as well, but they thought it was their little brother, Adam, until they realized he was still fast asleep.

Teresa's neighbor, who lived in the upstairs apartment, also heard mysterious footsteps while living there. He told Teresa he was sure that she was home one particular evening, because he heard someone walking up and down the stairs in her apartment. The footsteps and accompanying voices he heard were directly behind the wall in his hallway, which would have been right in Theresa's daughters' bedroom. But the children were spending the weekend at their father's house, and Teresa had gone out to dinner with friends that night. Still, the voices, in particular, had been very noticeable to him. The man's dog, he said, also barked at the same wall in his hallway, but he never found any logical explanation for the canine's irritating habit.

Cupboards opened and closed. An electric fan and the television malfunctioned. The TV turned itself on and off, or the channels changed while someone was trying to watch a show. Sometimes, Teresa became so frustrated with the ghostly game—jumping up to turn the TV back on, only to have it turn itself on just as she got to it—that she just unplugged the blasted thing and found something else to do. The ghost in charge of TV tampering wasn't on any better behavior when Theresa had company. It acted up even during daylight hours when Teresa had friends over. Her friends were shaken up a bit, but Teresa laughed about it, hoping it would keep them from thinking *she* was crazy, on account of her crazy TV.

When her youngest child, Adam, was six years old, he had a frightening experience and ended up sleeping with his mother for many nights in what was fast becoming the "family bed," as the paranormal incidents increased in frequency. The boy was on his way to his room to get his pajamas after his bath one night, when he saw a little girl in a dress walking slowly and deliberately up the stairs in front of him. He said she appeared out of nowhere and "her whole body was black like a shadow." She turned around and looked at him, glaring, as if she was annoyed that he dared to follow her up *her* stairs in *her* home. She was one angry little ghost. That's when Adam ran back down the stairs and begged his mother to let him sleep in her room. Teresa tried to tell him that ghosts don't get mad and can't hurt you, but she couldn't muster enough conviction in her own words to be at all convincing to her son. She and one of her daughters had seen the very same apparition in their dining room just a few days earlier when Adam was at his father's house. Nobody had told him about the incident, but Teresa could certainly empathize with what he was feeling, having just experienced it herself. The ghosts Teresa felt were intruders in her home were making her family feel as if *they* were the ones intruding!

Morgan and Michelle tried to console their young brother with a different approach. They had him place some crystal ornamental angels in his room for protection, and that actually seemed to work for a while. At least everyone felt safer—being surrounded by angels has that effect. But then the girls saw more evidence of ghosts in their own room, and the entire household was once again in a tizzy.

Teresa's daughters called to her several nights in a row after seeing "weird balls of light that floated in the air between the closet door and the bedroom door, not against the wall, but just hovering in the air." The girls were afraid to get out of bed and run downstairs to their mother, because the lights—or orbs in paranormal lingo—were too close to the door, and the sisters would have to go past them to get out into the hallway. In each case, the orbs simply hovered in place for a few moments before disappearing, so they didn't seem to be threatening in any way; but, their very presence was nonetheless intimidating. I mean, put yourself in their slippers. To experience a UFO sighting outside in broad daylight would be a little unnerving—especially if you ever saw *Fire in the Sky*! So imagine how frightening it would be to have Unidentified Flying Objects right *inside* your own home that are blocking your only escape route!

Startling as the orbs were, Morgan's climactic encounter with the dark and dusty young man in the kitchen was the final straw. Everyone in the family had had enough by then, and Teresa knew she had to do something. She couldn't call the police. They wouldn't be able to do anything—and might even have a good laugh before recommending a therapist to the distraught mother. She wasn't religious but had seen priests bless homes such as hers on TV, so she thought she'd give that a try. There didn't seem to be a lot of other options.

The priest she found had retired but was more than willing to help in any way he could. Teresa told him all of the things that had happened, and then he did a walk-through, blessing each and every room in the house. Teresa said the whole experience of having a priest bless her haunted home was like something out of a movie; but she figured, if it worked, it would be worth how silly she felt at the time. When he was finished, the priest sat Teresa and the children down and calmly told them that he felt several presences in the house and believed one of them was an evil one. He quickly added, however, that the blessing was *probably* enough to remedy the situation—the uncertainty in his voice, however, didn't exactly leave a warm, fuzzy feeling with the family. Still, it was better than nothing.

Things really were peaceful and without incident for a while in the Bender house. Teresa began to think that having a priest visit had actually done the trick, and everything would be okay after all. Then the noises started back up, and the cycle began all over again. *Every old house has its creaking, snapping, and clanging sounds, right? Maybe if they ignored them long enough, they would go away; or they would just get used to it. But then things began to happen that couldn't be ignored...*

She knew the drill. Teresa and her children soon moved out of the house and found an apartment they wouldn't have to share with any ghosts!

The Black Gloves
(and a Short Lesson on Symbolism)
Tupper Lake

Olivia was living in an apartment over an old store in downtown Tupper Lake when she saw something she could hardly believe, and she was certain nobody else would either. That's why, for many years, she kept quiet about it. Only her family and immediate friends were told. Then she read about others' experiences with the supernatural in *Haunted Northern New York* and its sequel and realized that strange, unexplainable things have happened to many of her North Country neighbors, and they're not afraid to talk about it, so why should she be?

In 1972 Olivia's family consisted of three children, a stepson, her husband and herself. They were living in the upstairs apartment until they could move into the home they'd bought in the spring. Her husband worked four to twelve at night, so she was alone with the children often until just past midnight. One evening, she and her son Todd were the only ones still awake. It was about 11 P.M., and she had pushed her bed over to the doorway so she and Todd could watch the TV that was in the living room. From that spot, they could see the living room and down the hallway to another bedroom and the bathroom. Olivia's attention was suddenly drawn toward the hallway door.

She said, "I glanced that way, and over the hallway door was a pair of black gloves—crossed over each other like a crucifix—that were hanging over the door." She'd never seen them before. She was so startled that she blurted out to her son, "Todd, look down the hall over the doorway!" He did, and he saw them too. Olivia jumped up and pushed the bed out of the doorway so she could get out of there, and Todd, who

53

was only eight years old, was hot on her heels, but the next time they looked back, the gloves were gone. Todd said, "Hey, they just disappeared!" The two huddled in bed, anxious for Olivia's husband to return from work.

Right on schedule, Todd arrived home about an hour later. Olivia heard him open and close the door downstairs and start upstairs. Then she heard him close the outside door and start up the stairs again. He did the same thing several times until, after about ten minutes of this behavior, Olivia had Todd go to the stairs and ask his stepfather what was wrong. Finally, he came all the way up to their apartment without stopping and going back down. Olivia, who was already a nervous wreck from her black glove ordeal, demanded to know what the problem was.

Her husband told her he came in the door as usual and started up the stairs. Then he looked back to make sure the outside door was closed, because, on the landing and going up the stairs behind him, there were footstep-like shadows coming in under the door. The best way he could describe it was to call them "shadow footsteps." It looked like someone was standing just behind the door. He kept going back down the stairs and looking out the door, because he wanted to find the source. He was certain there had to be a logical explanation for it, but none was ever found.

Thankfully, the shadow footsteps and the black gloves never returned. Olivia said, "Whatever was around that night must have gone back to where it came from." She doesn't even want to speculate on where that could have been. Though she still has no idea why she and Todd saw the black gloves, she firmly believes that it was something evil. But was it?

A lot of unexplained incidents have symbolic tendencies tied to them that play on either our own worst fears or on our innate desire to experience miracles. For example, if a crow pecks on your bedroom window, then death is said to be imminent for someone within. That's a common superstition that causes unnecessary fear, dread, and panic. I know, because it happened to me just before Halloween last year (of all times) and nobody has died yet. Crazy bird. But Hollywood has fed us so many lines about the evil crow and its power to foretell of impending death, that it has become ingrained in our psyches. The seeds of doubt and fear have been planted. Then, even when presented with information that should dispel such myths, we still can't help but worry that there might be something to it.

On the other hand, if you're sitting outside on the porch hoping to see a hummingbird—as I have also done—and suddenly one appears out of nowhere, hovering just inches before your face, looking you straight in the eye for a few magical moments, that must be a good sign, right? Our culture tells us that hummingbirds stand for pretty much everything nice—joy, magic, energy, wonder, etc. Knowing what I do about the meaning of symbols, the hummingbird incident was thrilling. The crow incident, on the other hand, was chilling. Both evoked emotions in me that were based on my own personal interpretation of the symbolism involved. But the same two symbols or incidents might have had different meanings for someone else, especially someone from a different culture.

Symbolism is very subjective, because different symbols mean different things to different people—so if you're looking for the message in something you believe is intended to be symbolic, you have to base it on your own individual circumstances and belief system at any given time.

As far as I'm concerned, in Olivia's case, the black gloves that were precisely laid over each other to form a cross above the doorway were rich in their symbolic meaning—if the message was from a spirit, as it may well have been. If you break it all down, black typically stands for the unknown, as well as something dark or evil. The cross symbolizes divine protection, because it can ward off evil. Gloves also symbolize protection from both the outdoors and from contact with others.

Symbolically, then, what Olivia saw may have meant that she and the children were being protected from contact with something evil that was trying to enter their home from outside and get to them. That's why the 'glove cross' appeared over the doorway—at the place of entrance. Her husband's experience a short time after Olivia's own frightening ordeal supports this explanation, because he actually saw whatever it was that was trying to enter their home, or at least he saw its shadow footsteps.

Henry David Thoreau (1817-1862) once said, "It's not what you look at that matters; it's what you see." And if you can't see past outside appearances, you may completely miss the intended message.

—

The British Are Coming!

Hopkinton

Photo by Author

The historic McCargar residence, Hopkinton

On the last of February, 1814, after the British party had returned from their incursion to Malone, and had arrived at French Mills, they learned from a citizen-spy...that a large amount of flour belonging to the United States Army was stored in a barn in the village of Hopkinton, and that there was no guard at that place to protect it.

Thirty soldiers, who proceeded in sleighs, arrived at that place early in the morning before the inhabitants were up. They first posted sen-

tinels at the door of every house, and proceeded to search for arms in every place where they might be suspected to be found, and succeeded in obtaining about twenty stand, which had been distributed among the inhabitants. It is said that several muskets were saved by being hastily laid in a bed, which had been occupied but a few moments previous, and thus eluded the search that was made for them. Their case has been described by the poet:

> "'Tis odd, not one of all of these seekers thought,
> And seems to me almost a sort of blunder,
> Of looking *in* the bed as well as *under*."

They found some three hundred barrels of flour stored in a barn owned by Judge Hopkins, and occupied by Dr. Sprague, but having no teams for conveying away more than half of that quantity, they began to destroy the remainder, but being dissuaded by the inhabitants, they desisted, and distributed the remainder among the citizens.

—"War of 1812," Hough's *History of St. Lawrence and Franklin Counties*, 1852

At the center of excitement on that historic morning was the home and office of Dr. Gideon Sprague, one of Hopkinton's earliest settlers and its second physician. The two-and-a-half-story home is located at 2831 State Highway 11B, adjacent to the village's museum and park, and is now owned by Jared and Maureen McCargar. At one time, the barn that was raided in the above account stood in the McCargar's backyard, but that wasn't all. Their backyard was also the local cemetery for a good many years—in fact, it was likely there from the time the first settlers settled the land in 1803. Judge Isaac Hopkins, the founder of the town, was the owner of the property containing the cemetery until it was acquired by Dr. Sprague in 1814—house, barn, and burial ground. Dr. Sprague lived and practiced medicine in that house until his passing in 1859, and he was also the St. Lawrence county coroner in 1834, so the graveyard between the house and the barn was in a convenient location for a while, until there wasn't room for any more graves. In 1840 the cemetery was dug up and moved around the corner to the sprawling Hopkinton-Fort Jackson Cemetery on County Road 49.

Most people agree that it's best not to disturb the dead on sacred ground, but sometimes you have no choice. At such times, you may be quite certain you've moved everything in sight, but you can never be certain you've moved those things that are *not* in sight. Invariably, something gets left behind, and sometimes that something is some*one*. That's not to say that whoever is haunting the McCargar residence at the present time is a straggler from the cemetery that was once on their land. But it certainly remains one of several possibilities.

The McCargars purchased their historic home in 1999 and began renovating it at once. I should point out that renovating an old home is another well-known trigger that tends to awaken the dead. There's no reason to avoid renovating, though. Just be prepared to see an increase in paranormal activity, if your home is predisposed to such, because changes to the environment tend to bring out curious spirits of past residents. Maureen admits that a lot of strange things have happened since they moved in, especially since they began renovations.

A couple of years ago, during a period of especially heavy remodeling, Maureen and Jared were sitting on the couch in their living room when they both felt something distinctly "whoosh" by right in front of them. Jared said it felt like he was a spectator at a silent track meet, he could feel the breeze of someone zoom past him. Whatever it was, it made a believer out of the skeptical man. There was no chance that it had been a draft or breeze, because no doors or windows were open at the time. Perhaps the good doctor (Sprague), grabbed his medical bag and flew toward the door on an urgent house call. The McCargars think their living room may have been the actual office of Dr. Sprague, because it is located at the front of the home, overlooking the street— and because it seems to be the center of paranormal activity.

Maureen is certain that the spirit of a woman is involved, too, because she saw a mystery woman up close and personal. One night when a friend was sleeping over, Maureen was lying in bed (her bedroom is right above the living room) when she looked up to see a figure in the doorway. She described it as a lady wearing a long dress that was "gathered like a prairie dress," and her hair was in a bun. She saw her very clearly and said it looked like an actual solid person standing in the hallway, the way anyone would look in the glow of the nightlight. She was not transparent or fuzzy—she was as clear as could be. Thinking it was her friend, she asked, "Did you need something?" Nobody answered, and just about the time the figure turned and walked away, it donned on her that her friend didn't dress like that or wear her hair in a bun! The next morning her friend confirmed that it definitely wasn't her.

So who was it? It's hard to say, because so many people have come and gone and lived and presumably died in the home. Dr. Sprague's first wife, Maria (Pier), died there in 1826, when she was just thirty-four years old. She had given birth to five children in the home. At the time of her death, the youngest was only two, and the oldest was twelve. Dr. Sprague then married her sister, Laura (Pier), who helped raise her nieces and nephews. Laura passed away in 1834 at the age of forty-three. Dr. Sprague and his last wife (Rhoda Kent) took in at least two children from another family—Fidelia and Egnert Sanford. They were among the thirteen children of the widower Samuel Stickney Sanford who died in 1846. Dr. Sprague died in 1859; and his wife Rhoda died twenty-one years later. Upon Dr. Sprague's death, his son Dr. F.P. Sprague, succeeded him in his practice; possibly practicing out of his father's office in the Sprague family home. So, as you can see, between family members and patients, there's no doubt that many people passed through the doors of the Sprague house over the years. Sadly, for some it would be where they took their last breath.

Sometimes when Maureen and Jared are sitting in the living room, they hear the sound of footsteps going around the bed on the floor above them. It's a very distinctive sound on the old wooden floors. And Jared's mother has felt someone climb into bed with her in the guest bedroom on three or four different occasions. She babysits often and has spent many nights in the home, especially when Maureen was on bed rest at the end of her last pregnancy. She finally told whoever it was to "go to the Light" (Heaven) and hasn't had a similar experience since.

Another spirit seems to watch over the youngsters in the McCargar household. The most likely person would be the aforementioned Maria Pier Sprague, or her sister, Laura. Maybe the female apparition Maureen encountered was one of them. Maternal instincts seem to transcend all boundaries, even that between life and death, based on my knowledge of local paranormal cases involving female apparitions watching over infants and small children. And, certainly, both of the Pier-Sprague sisters showed strong mothering instincts.

The room that is now the McCargar's son Sammie's used to be the spare room, and it was always the coldest room in the house. The McCargars could see their breath in the empty room, even if they opened the bedroom door so that the heat from the rest of the house could help to warm it. But they were never able to get it warmed up—that is, until they moved Sammie, now three, into the room. Since then, someone has been tampering with the thermostat, as if they're trying to keep it at a balmy eighty degrees for the little boy's sake—but that's a tad too balmy, even for an adaptable toddler. It's a far cry from the see-your-breath atmosphere in that room before. The McCargars also pointed out that the curtains on the room's window were always being adjusted before Sammie was born, as if someone kept opening and closing them.

A child ghost may also remain in the home. Who it could be is anybody's guess, considering the house's rich history. In the upstairs bathroom, Maureen once felt someone tap her on the shoulder at the same moment that she heard the voice of a small child. She turned around expecting to see Sammie, but nobody was there. Sammie was down for his nap, and it definitely couldn't have been Carson—he was merely an infant at the time! Both Maureen and Jared also clearly heard a young child's voice on several disturbing occasions in different rooms in the house. Sometimes it says, "Mommy," and sometimes they can't understand what it's saying, but they're positive it's the voice of a young child.

One of the ghosts is responsible for finding a way to turn on toys that, by all rights, should not be able to turn on. Sometimes the only way to stop the noise from the toys is to remove their batteries, which is what Maureen did to a number of the toys. However, since then some of those same toys have been heard! The first time it happened, Maureen investigated to ensure that she had, in fact, taken the batteries out of a certain toy. She had, so it was impossible, but the toy somehow operated without them. This is a surprisingly common phenomenon in haunted houses. Don't ask me how they do it, but somehow ghosts can manipulate energy to make the inoperable operate, if only for a moment. It's like a crack of lightning in a powerful thunderstorm that causes objects to turn on for a second. I can say from personal experience that you don't want to hear a doll start singing a lullaby out of the blue in the middle of a storm when the lights are out!

Sammie has told his mother that someone was playing with his toys in his room. Since children sense spirit far better than adults, I'm never too quick to assume that it's the old "imaginary friend" trick. What if—at least in some cases—they're not so imaginary, after all? A coworker told me his brother who lives in the town of Jefferson in the Catskills was remodeling the old farmhouse he'd purchased a few years ago. When he pulled off a sheet of paneling, there was a very unusual name etched into the plaster beneath—the same exact name his three-year-old daughter had mentioned several times since they moved in. Her parents assumed she was going through an imaginary friend stage when she talked about the person with the strange name. But can an imaginary friend write on walls? Can *imaginary* friends turn off the nightlight after you fall asleep? That's what often happens in Sammie's room, and the nightlight is placed too high for the toddler to reach.

There are imaginary friends—figments of children's imaginations that are very common and normal. Child psychologists agree that it should be neither encouraged nor discouraged, that children will eventually outgrow them. Then there are imaginary friends that seem not to really be imaginary—they may be actual ghosts, spirits, guardian angels, or spirit guides. Some adults would rather say their child has an imaginary friend than to entertain the possibility that it might be a ghost or an angel. In the latter case, the so-called imaginary friend either watches over the child or simply enjoys being in the child's company, for whatever reason. If other things have taken place in your home that can't be explained, or even if they haven't, you should still consider that your child's imaginary friend may not be imaginary at all. It may be very real—but as harmless as if it *were* imaginary.

In the McCargar's wonderful home with its colorful past, it seems there are at least two or three spirits—the mother, the young child, and the marathon runner (or the physician racing to an emergency house call)! Maybe they stayed behind when the cemetery was relocated, or maybe they were drawn back by a strong instinct. Maybe they are spirit guardians passing for imaginary friends. We'll probably never know who haunts the house. But they sure make its history all the more exciting.

The House on Murphy Road

Norwood

Joshua's most disturbing paranormal experience occurred when he was visiting friends in Rochester several years ago. He knew that a lady had been murdered a few years earlier—stabbed to death—in the apartment directly below the bedroom he was to sleep in. But sleep wouldn't find him that night. In fact, the evening had something else in mind for him altogether.

His eyes were closed, yet he was wide awake. Beneath his lids, his eyes focused on a light that cast a bluish glow. In a split second, the blue light was transformed into the end of a shovel, with a bloodied blade. A stream of blood hit the end of the shovel then curved over—in painfully slow motion—and hit the end again. The next vision was of a woman going to the bedroom door, opening it, and saying angrily to the visitor, "What do you want?" Then the stabbing began, right there at the door. Joshua witnessed (in his mind) an event that had occurred five years earlier. It wasn't a ghost, per se, but oftentimes people who live in haunted houses have similar visions. In fact, visions of previous murders in haunted houses are often seen by more than one individual, as a spontaneous mental image while they are awake, or in vivid dreams. It's a form of clairvoyancy.

Four or five years ago, Joshua lived in a big old house on Murphy Road in Norwood. He was up late one night—it was about 3 A.M.—and he went into the kitchen. Just as he went through the door, he saw what he described as "an aura that looked like it sat down at the table." It seemed to pull up a chair, the body was bent at the waist, the hands gripped the seat, and the head lowered over the table. He knew it was his grandmother who had passed when he was only three or four. It's not that it looked particularly like her, because it was only a hazy outline. But he felt certain of who it was, and he always trusts his senses.

Joshua and his mother have both seen 'smoke' that they believe was spirit energy in their home on Murphy Road. The boy was putting dishes away in the kitchen and had just walked out when he saw "big puffs of smoke" that instantly vanished. His mother saw similar energy in the living room once when she was eating breakfast. Smoke-like mist was coming from the recliner, and it drifted over to a picture before vanishing.

There've been a lot of other strange things, as well, but that's how it is when you come from a family of psychics, like Joshua does. For example, Joshua once encountered an angry little red orb at summer school. It was during an Earth Science class at Massena Central High School that he saw the orb darting back and forth, at one time almost hitting him. (That's one way to keep the students awake in class!) Another incident happened at a local movie theater. Joshua needed something to get his mind off a health scare, so he and his mother went to see "Brother Bear." When he went into the bathroom at the cinema, he felt a distinct finger run down his back. Joshua still has no idea who touched him in the bathroom; he didn't see anyone else in there. But the theater is rumored to be haunted by the ghosts of a hand—holding little boy and girl who were once seen walking into one of its cinemas before vanishing into thin air.

The bathroom at Joshua's house on Murphy Road has been the scene of several paranormal incidents. His mother was taking a shower one day and had just stepped out of the tub when the water turned back on. Like Joshua, she felt quite certain that it was just her deceased mother, so she calmly said, "Hi, Mom." Just as she did, the water turned back off.

Joshua's own bathtub incident was a little more disturbing. It was two in the morning when he decided to take a bath. He was checking the water temperature and heard a feminine voice say something. He panicked, thinking it was his mother and not wanting to be caught uncovered. So he quickly wrapped a towel around himself and went out to see who it was. His mother was fast asleep. Yet the voice he heard had been very close and very clear. Needless to say, it didn't set the tone for a relaxing bath!

The family has since moved from Murphy Road to Raquette Road in Potsdam. Joshua reported to me that the incense he burns in his room has been snuffing out, and his window blind occasionally opens, often in conjunction with the incense going out. He does not keep his window open, so it can't be blamed on a draft or breeze. The hot water in the faucet upstairs turns itself on several times a day, inexplicably. So, the paranormal incidents certainly seem to have followed the family to their new home...right up to Joshua's bedroom window, in fact!

The teen recently found large footprints in the snow, starting in the middle of the yard and leading right up to his window. But there were no tracks leading away from it. It looks like someone went in—but hasn't come out.

The House on Urban Drive

Massena

Strange things started happening in a house on Urban Drive as soon as a young couple moved in with their two children in the mid-eighties. The house was built in 1956, but their land has been occupied for much longer. At one time in the early 1800s, it was part of the historic subdivision of "Mile Square" known as "Indian Reservation," and in 1899, their property was known as the "Clary Farm." In fact, all of Urban Drive was farmland at the turn of the century. The neighbors across the street even dug up old cow bones during construction of their house. But it isn't some cow that's haunting the homes on Urban Drive now! It may be an old cowboy or a farm hand, though.

The first incident involved the suspended ceiling in the master bedroom. Dick and Jane (not their real names) heard heavy footsteps overhead—on their ceiling! So they removed the ceiling tiles, giving them a clear view of the solid ceiling above. The was no sign of anything out of the ordinary, but they decided they would sleep better knowing they didn't have to worry about something lurking overhead that they couldn't see. Little did they know that there were plenty of other ways they would be kept up at night. Not only did they have a newborn and a three-year-old; but they also had a ghost that was acting like a child.

One time, in the dead of winter, the couple was awakened around 3 A.M., by voices just outside their bedroom window. They couldn't tell if the voices were male or female or young or old, but they were definitely voices—just somehow muffled. Dick got up to check it out. It was an extremely calm night, so the thirty-degree air was very still. There

67

were no footprints in the fresh snow under their window or anywhere in the backyard.

Another time, pounding on the back door roused the couple in the early morning hours, but nobody was there. The same thing happened on the front door several days later in the middle of the afternoon, but nobody was there, either. That time, however, Jane was standing right near the front door when the knocking occurred, so the perpetrator couldn't have gotten away without being seen, unless it was invisible....

Several times, the couple thought one of their children had awakened and was out of bed, because they saw white shadows go by out of the corners of their eyes while they were lying in bed watching TV. When they got up to look in on them, though, the children were always asleep. Many paranormal incidents have been experienced simultaneously by both Dick and Jane. More recently, however, each has had their share of individual experiences.

Dick is into reloading handguns, and he does it in the basement at night when everyone is asleep, because "it's a serious thing—and you need to concentrate." One day he came home from work at about 11:30 P.M. and looked in on the kids before heading to the basement. He needed to know that everyone was asleep, so he wouldn't be disturbed. About a half hour later, as he was reloading shells, he heard the faucet turn on in the bathroom upstairs, which meant someone was up. But the water kept running and never stopped. When he finally went upstairs to see what was going on, he found the bathroom sink about to overflow with the water still running and the bathroom all steamed up. He turned it off and went to see who was awake, but everyone was in exactly the same position they were in when he had checked on them just a half hour earlier.

A few days later, the couple was across the street visiting with neighbors on their porch, and they told them about the strange incident with the bathroom sink. They had a feeling that the neighbors weren't completely buying it and felt a little silly for even mentioning it. When suppertime came, they left their neighbors' and went back to their own house to eat. Seconds later, the phone rang. It was the same neighbors, telling them excitedly that they'd just gone inside and found their own bathroom sink running! Nobody had been inside the neighbors' house the whole time the two couples were visiting.

The next most memorable incident involved the television set. The family's TV was an old floor model. It didn't work by remote control; it had the push/pull knob. One day the TV turned off while Jane was watching it, so she got up and turned it back on. Thinking there might be a short in the outlet, she moved the TV to the wall on the opposite side of the living room. That didn't help—it still turned off by itself a couple of times a month. Finally, one night when she'd had quite enough, she 'talked to it' (assuming it was a ghost) and told it to leave her TV on. When that didn't work, she went into the bedroom and warned it not to go in there and touch the bedroom television. Many ghosts will listen, but not this one!

While Jane was lying at the foot of the bed watching TV, it turned off. This time, she was armed with a remote control, so she easily turned it back on. But it kept turning off as soon as she turned it on. At last, she screamed in a fit of frustration that awakened her husband, and she handed him the remote. He proceeded to be drawn into the same bizarre game. It must have been the game of the day, though, because it never happened again. Instead, the ghost moved on to something noisier and more alarming—the smoke alarm.

There are six smoke alarms in the home—and all of them are well-maintained and working properly. But one night, the smoke alarm in the dining room went off at 2 or 3 A.M., waking everyone up. They searched anxiously for the source of the suspected smoke; but since there was no smoke to be found, there was obviously no source of smoke either. It was as if someone had reached up and pressed the test button, manually setting off the alarm. That, too, was a solitary incident.

For a long time, a Tupperware cup was kept on the back of the kitchen sink for quick sips. One time in the middle of the night, there was a loud clunk in the kitchen. The next morning, the Tupperware cup was sitting in the middle of the kitchen floor. The children were too little to have reached it, and there were no pets at the time to blame it on.

Just last year, Jane was sitting at the table in the kitchen talking to her mother on the phone when an orange juice container flew past her and landed on the floor a good seven or eight feet from where it had been on the counter. It was mid-morning, and she was the only one home. She gasped and said, "Oh, my God!" Her mother—on the other end of the line—asked her what was going on. She then told Jane that she could hear the thud of the container hitting the floor even over the phone. If it had somehow fallen off the counter, it wouldn't have flown through the air like a missile. It would have landed on the floor beneath the counter, but it didn't. It literally projected across the entire length of the kitchen.

Others have also sensed something fishy going on in the house. The family's Tabby 'owned' one corner of the couch when he was alive. It was his spot, and he always slept there. But once, when the family had been away for the day, they returned home to find him peeking out from a chair near the front door, staring at the couch which was several feet away. His ears were flat, as if he was either very frightened or very angry, and he wouldn't budge from his spot. The poor cat spent a good part of the day glaring at the couch, like his worst enemy was sitting there taunting him. Finally, Dick picked the cat up and tossed him light- ly onto his spot to see if he would settle down and stop acting strange- ly. But just as the cat's paws touched the couch, it sprang back off with a hiss. The last thing the Tabby wanted was a catnap when his spot was obviously being so rudely occupied by someone else.

A friend who was visiting the couple one time became uneasy while sitting in the living room and pointedly asked the couple if they believed in ghosts. They'd never discussed the topic before with him, and he was unfamiliar with their experiences, but he said he sensed a spirit in their house. He felt it was benevolent—mischievous perhaps, but not harm- ful. That didn't make it any easier to swallow what would happen next.

Jane was sitting at the computer playing a game when she heard a voice say, "Send it down." She'd played the same game many times, and it never had talked back! But the voice didn't come from her computer, it came from across the room, directly behind her. She said the voice was very "slow and creepy." She would have dismissed it, but she heard it again ten minutes later. Her oldest child came in and could tell that his mother was upset. She told him what happened and asked if he or his father had come in from the garage, but they hadn't. Her son searched the entire house for a possible source of sound like that, but nothing could explain it. Even the intercom from the garage had been unplugged. The television was off, and so was the radio. The computer game has sound but not voices. There simply was no reasonable explanation.

Her son waited to see if it would happen again, but he finally gave up and went back out in the garage and told his father he'd better go inside. Mom seemed a bit distraught. She really thought the two of them had been playing a practical joke on her. Not five minutes after her son went back out in the garage, the voice said the same thing again! She was perplexed. That night while lying in bed, Jane tried to get Dick to admit it was him, but finally she conceded that it wasn't. That's when it really hit her. For the first time, she was actually scared and started to cry. She never heard anyone say those three words again or figured out what they could have meant. But she did hear the same *voice* again.

A cryptic message was left on the family's answering machine recently, and it wasn't by accident. Their pre-recorded message clearly states whose home the caller has reached. But the raspy voice on the recording said very deliberately, "How'd I do?" That was it. That was all. Whoever heard of a ghost seeking reassurance? It sounded like an old man —a hillbilly. It was just like the voice she had heard while she was at the computer that day—slow and creepy; with a bit of a twang. They kept the message on their machine for a few weeks before finally erasing it.

For the most part, the entire family takes the ghost thing pretty lightly. They accept it and work around it. It's not like their ghost is causing *too* much trouble—at least not so far. Maybe he's waiting for them to answer his question, "How'd I do?," before he plans his next move.

The Night of the Light Show

Russell

Barry Strate had a wonderful watchdog when he lived in Russell. But one night the dog stood at the top of the stairs looking down and growling—something he seldom did—and he refused to go down the stairs, which was very unusual. Normally, the dog "stormed downstairs barking at any sound he deemed out of the ordinary." Not so, when there's a ghost in residence.

Barry told me of the house he grew up in, known around town as the Teepell House, for the doctor who once owned the place. It no longer stands, but the Strate family lived there for twenty-some years and had a number of strange incidents occur to them in the sixties and seventies.

I always explain to audiences how sensitive cats and dogs are to a spirit world we may not even be aware of. As an example, I often share an incident regarding a cat that was too frightened to continue up the stairs in an old haunted apartment building on Laurel Avenue in Massena. When the owner called to her cat because it was behaving so strangely, it slowly backed down the stairs, its ears flattened like wings. It never turned its head or broke eye contact with whatever was at the top of the stairs. Granted, cats chase the light shining from flashlights, and dogs chase their tails, but this was something beyond the usual crazy behavior of our pets. Besides, usually there are other mysterious things going on in these places, so the behavior of the pets confirms their owners' worst fears—they have a ghost!

Barry and his mother, Eileen, occasionally felt someone tapping them on their shoulders when they stood at the kitchen sink. They heard noises that seemed to come from the attic. "Probably squirrels," Barry would say, but his mother always added teasingly, "Or old Doc Teepell." One time when Barry and his sister were home alone during a severe thunderstorm, they were heading upstairs when the attic door that adjoined the stairwell suddenly blew open with such a force, Barry thought it had come unhinged. Could squirrels do *that*?

While Barry's father missed most of these events because he worked nights, he did happen to be home the night of the mysterious light show. He and Eileen were watching TV when, all of a sudden, a ball of misty light originating near the front door shot straight across the living room toward the corner where Eileen was sitting. Just before it reached her, it abruptly shifted direction and "darted about erratically in front of the mantle for a bit." Then the ball of light disappeared into an opening on the other side of the fireplace. Barry's parents both watched it, completely stunned. His father tore the mantle apart, looking for a cause, but found nothing that could explain it. There had been no traffic coming down the road at the time, so it couldn't have been car lights; but it was a show they'd never forget.

There was also another house in Russell that Barry had heard was haunted. Like the Teepell House, it was an old, historic home, but one that no longer stands. Most of the local townspeople are familiar with the stories of a face that had been seen in the second-floor window of the house, even though the home was vacant for years. A volunteer fireman was probably the last person to see the face, because he saw it the day the house burned down. Joe said he was running the tanker on his second or third trip around the burning house, when he looked up and saw an old bearded guy in the window, surrounded by flames. Even though he knew it was impossible, because there was no actual floor left on the second floor of the house at that point for anyone to conceivably stand on, he still ran over to the other firefighters and said, "Hey, what's that guy doing up there?" But by then, the face was gone.

The old man in the window has long since vanished, but his story, like many other ghost stories, will probably endure.

The Odd Fellows Lodge

Redwood

Photo by Author

The Odd Fellows Lodge, Redwood

Jon Scheer belongs to the Odd Fellows Lodge in Redwood, New York. The building is a combination of the original structure and a church that was added on later. Upstairs is a gameroom where the brothers gather for friendly card-playing and such after meetings.

One night Jon and his friend, George, were in the middle of a friendly game of pool when they were interrupted by the sound of whispering. It was a little strange, but nature called, so George went downstairs alone to use the bathroom. When he came back up, he said, "Very funny, rattling the doorknob like that, Jon." But Jon had never left the upstairs. It was one of several baffling incidents that have taken place in the old building.

Another night when Jon and George were playing cards at the lodge, George again went downstairs to use the bathroom. This time when he returned, he told Jon that he had seen a shadow on the wall ahead of him, as if someone was standing between the light and him. It seemed that every time George excused himself to use the bathroom, something paranormal happened! (Maybe it's not so crazy for women to visit the powder room in pairs, after all. Laugh if you must, but at least there's safety in numbers!)

The last notable incident at the Odd Fellows Lodge happened one evening after a meeting, when pennies fell out of the ceiling during a game of poker. Jon explained that whenever he and the brothers take change out of their pockets to play poker, they automatically toss the unwanted pennies up into the open space where a ceiling panel came loose in the game room. On that particular night, while five of the men sat playing cards, the pennies came shooting out of the ceiling—it was like pennies from Heaven! But it wasn't as if the ceiling was collapsing and the pennies were all sliding down in one spot. They were literally shooting out of the ceiling, quite intentionally. Someone 'up there' must have thought the men should be holding onto their pennies (or spending their loose change on other things!).

Whoever haunts the Odd Fellows Lodge seems to be a fun-loving practical jokester, so nothing will change on account of a possible ghost among the brothers. The men will continue holding meetings; they'll still play poker after those meetings and toss pennies up into the ceiling; and George will continue answering to the call of nature, fearlessly undeterred by strange whispering, shadows on the wall, and doorknobs jangling in the bathroom.

The Pennysaver

Massena

Home of 'The Pennysaver,' *Massena*

When Tom Griffis purchased the old house at 305 Main Street, at the corner of St. Regis Boulevard and Main, he hired a local contractor to convert it into an attractive, light gray office building. But the settling of the sheetrock dust and the silencing of the familiar sounds of construction heralded in a new set of disturbances in the converted building—unexplained noises, hot-headed ghosts, and a specter with a penchant for toys.

It all began when *The Pennysaver* staff started moving the computers for their production crew into the newly remodeled attic on the third floor—they had been set up in the basement previously. Since then, employees have heard the doors on the third floor click and open several times a day when the rooms up there are supposedly empty. Footsteps have been heard by past and current employees, on weekends and evenings when they were working alone. One former employee said she occasionally heard a radio playing on the third floor while she was working elsewhere in the building, even though she was the only one there. Various subtleties in the atmosphere indicated something paranormal was going on.

Not so subtle was the day in the attic when Venna Hillman, the manager, actually had a closet door yanked out of her hand. She had a grip on the handle and had opened it partway when it suddenly slammed shut with a violent jerk, as if someone gave it a hardy pull to prevent her from opening it further. But the third floor is not the only place where mysterious happenings have been experienced at *The Pennysaver*.

On the first floor, Max the dog whiles his days away chomping on his favorite squeak toy, but it seems that someone's been toying with the staff when the dog isn't there. Several times employees have been upstairs when they've heard the yellow toy start squeaking and, after checking, have found the first floor vacant, with nothing out of place to account for the unmistakable sound. The toy just lays there undisturbed next to the printer, looking as guilty as sin. Obviously, it's impossible that it could have squeaked on its own. One of the employees heard the crazy, possessed toy go off one time when he was working in the basement, and it was so loud that it sounded like it was right next to him. Max wasn't there at the time, but his toy was—right up alongside the printer on the first floor where he'd last chewed on it.

The same employee stumbled upon a nosy ghost with his hands in the file cabinets on the first floor. The employee was the last one out that night and was just heading down the stairs to go when he heard a file cabinet drawer close nearby, as if someone was going through the drawers. But nobody was physically there. Though that employee is still somewhat skeptical about the building being haunted, he admitted that he, too, has heard unexplained footsteps going up and down the stairs from time to time.

Curious to know who's been haunting them and why, *The Pennysaver* invited a renowned psychic and paranormal investigator, Belle Salisbury, to tour the premises. Her findings helped to explain a lot. As a psychic investigator, she sees and communicates with any spirits present. She brought up an interesting point. Alleged hauntings don't always indicate the presence of actual ghosts—as in earthbound souls that are unable to rest. She feels many cases of hauntings are actually just the living tapping into another dimension in another time, which is why the so-called ghosts often seem to be going about their business, unaware of our presence. It's difficult to sum up in a couple of sentences a concept that really could fill an entire book. But, simply put, we hear them and sometimes see them, and we feel their presence, as they do very regular things in their own place and time, because for a brief moment, we are on the "same wavelength" as the so-called 'ghosts.'

At any rate, what Belle saw in her mind's eye, was quite detailed and very interesting. On the first floor, she immediately sensed an older gentleman—possibly a bit feeble-minded, but very jovial and kind. He puttered around the building, and played with the dog. In fact, he showed an affinity for Max and indicated that he squeaks the pampered pup's toys to get the dog's attention. That explains why employees often hear the toys squeaking when nobody is around, including Max. The man Belle saw is very quiet and unassuming and called himself 'the keeper.' There was also a younger man with his sleeves casually rolled up, as if he was getting right down to business (whatever that business was). He had very dark, thick, slick hair and wore a mustache.

The presence of a young woman was felt on the second floor, which Belle believed had been the actual living quarters at one time. The woman seemed somewhat 'catered to' and didn't really do anything particular around the house. She wore a long, old fashioned dress and held a parasol. An older woman's presence was felt, as well. She seemed to take care of the home. No presence was felt on the third floor, where many of the paranormal incidents have occurred, but Belle looked out of the window overlooking Main Street and noted that it had been farmland and stables, and only one of the two main roads at that intersection existed. (St. Regis Boulevard wasn't constructed until the 1950s.) She saw a number of very tall trees lining the street side of the property.

Moving down into the basement, Belle felt the farmhands had entered through the side door of the building, where they were greeted by a split-level stairway that led down into the basement and up into the kitchen. They were required to go down into the basement to wash up before being allowed upstairs to eat.

Also in the basement, Belle had a strong feeling that there had been something buried in the crawl space beneath the first floor, accessed through what is now the bathroom. She felt it was simply a document or something that personally identified the person who left it there. Someone many years ago thought it would be neat to leave something for someone else to find one day. It was nothing necessarily of value; just something of personal interest.

Several days after Venna and I met with Belle and her husband, Gary, I visited the Massena Museum. With the help of Theresa Sharp, Town Historian, I was able to dig up some background information on the Balch family, who I believe lived at that location in the 1800s and early 1900s. First, I confirmed that Route 37 (St. Regis Boulevard) had not been there during the family's tenure. In fact, the whole area at the current intersection of Route 37 and Main Street was farmland for a very long time. Fred P. Balch was a farmer, a County Superintendent of the Poor, and an innkeeper. He took in boarders who were looking for a room while enjoying the therapeutic waters of the nearby Massena Springs. The Springs were once highly marketable, due to the sulphur in the waters of the Racquette River at that location that seemed to cure so many ailments in the nineteenth and early twentieth centuries.

According to the 1870 St. Lawrence County census, Fred Balch's wife, Elvira, kept house. Their son, also Fred P., became a cabinet maker on the premises; his wife Ellie, who was twenty-one at the time, had no occupation listed, but they did have a baby named Fred Junior who she must have tended to. There were two domestic servants, Malinda (sixteen) and Sarah (twenty-one); and there were likely several farmhands to help around the large farm. The younger Fred P. recalled having to sleep in the granary when the family's rooms were all taken by boarders (*Massena Observer—August 20, 1936*). While his father was boarding people at their own three-story home, the younger Fred P. was busy keeping up with the demand for the water at the springs by working at the famous Hatfield House, built in 1872. In those days, many area homes were opened to boarders who arrived by stagecoach by the hundreds just to visit Massena Springs.

My findings at the museum complemented Belle's findings nicely. If Belle was glimpsing the Balch family during her investigation, then Fred Balch Sr. may have been 'the keeper' of his boarding house and of the records for his job as Superintendent of the Poor. If he was keeping records, he may also have been the one who was heard opening and closing file cabinet drawers in the building. The young man with his sleeves rolled up that Belle saw could have been the younger Fred P., the cabinet maker. The coddled young lady may have been his wife. The older woman undoubtedly had her hands full caring for her family, as well as boarders—and that woman might have been Elvira Balch, listed as "Keeping House" on the 1870 census.

On a large farm, such as the Balch's, stables and plentiful farmland would have been a given, especially since the only mode of transportation at the time was horse-and-buggy and stagecoach. And Venna and Tom agreed that there had been very tall trees across the front of the house/building when it was purchased in 1990.

There were no negative feelings noted at all during Belle's investigation, just positive ones. Most of the staff at *The Pennysaver* believes that there is probably a harmless ghost (or several) in residence, and the investigation and historical data seems to support that. So, keep that in mind the next time you stop in to place an ad in the weekly paper. Don't pry open any stubborn closet doors or step on stray squeak toys. You never know whose space you might be invading!

The Phantom of Kendrew Corners

DeKalb

Approaching the bridge at Kendrew Corners, DeKalb

It was 1955. The night was foggy along the Oswegatchie, so the man in the 1947 Chevy convertible was only going about twenty-five miles per hour when he crossed the bridge on Route 812 at Kendrew Corners on his way to a dance in nearby Hermon. The debonair man sporting a bow tie and white shirt appeared out of nowhere and stepped directly into the path of the slow-moving vehicle—and looked the twenty-year-old driver square in the eye at the moment of impact. The five young people in the Chevy stared in disbelief and horror as the man simply fell backwards, straight as an arrow. They jumped from the car with flashlights, expecting the worst, but the man was gone. How could that be?

They had all seen the older gentleman and watched the seemingly rehearsed scene as it was played out in front of them. He had stepped out, as if on purpose, directly in front of the approaching car. He looked at them, as if he'd been expecting them, or even waiting for them. And then he fell back, without a sound. He was wearing a tuxedo, a black cape lined with red satin, and an old-style black felt hat—like something out of the twenties or thirties. In fact, he looked like he was coming straight from a costume ball! His appearance was unforgettable, yet he wasn't there. They could find no sign of him anywhere—no blood stains on the pavement, no dent on the car, no trail at the side of the road where he had dragged his broken body off into the woods. Still, they searched the woods, just in case. Nothing.

The bewildered friends relived the incident second by second and suddenly realized something. At the moment of impact, there actually hadn't been any impact! They hadn't felt the thud of the man's body against the car. They hadn't heard a thud. They just saw the car hit a man silently, and they watched him fall backwards. In hindsight, it had been surreal. Nobody would have fallen back like that if struck by a car, like the strangely-dressed man had been. The man they thought they hit should have slumped over the hood or been thrown up into the air.

They finally came to the conclusion that they had encountered a suicidal phantom. Crazy as it sounded, there was no other explanation they could think of. If they had gone to the police, they thought they would have been told they were crazy. Instead, they waited to see if anyone was reported missing or found injured or dead in the area for the next few days, but no such report ever came. And they really hadn't expected that it would. The more they thought about it, the more they realized they'd encountered a ghost.

Let's go back. It was 1982. The night was foggy along the Oswegatchie, so the flashy Riley sports car was only going about twenty-five miles per hour when it approached the bridge at Kendrew Corners on Route 812 on its way to Ogdensburg. The debonaire man sporting a bow tie and white shirt appeared out of nowhere and stepped directly into the path of the slow-moving sports car-looking the twenty-year-old driver square in the eye at the moment of impact. The young man in the Riley stared in disbelief and horror as the man he struck simply fell backwards, straight as an arrow. He jumped from the car, expecting the worst, but the man was gone. *How could that be...*

After searching everywhere, the frantic young man raced to his father's house. The father said his son was as white as a ghost when he blurted out that he'd hit a guy and searched for him but couldn't find him anywhere. *Flashback*. His father was back in 1955, and the details of that awful night resurfaced in his mind. He asked his son if the man had been wearing a bow tie and cape and looked like he was coming from a costume ball. His son was speechless as he nodded. How could his father have possibly known? The same thing had happened to him, that's how. Incredibly, both had been the same age and were at the same spot when they encountered the phantom at Kendrew Corners. Neither could find any sign of the man they were certain they'd hit. It was bizarre. What are the odds that two members of the same family would experience the same chilling incident—both when they were precisely twenty years old? I'd say pretty slim. And yet, that's just what happened.

I wonder how many young men will encounter the phantom near the bridge at Kendrew Corners in their twentieth year. He seems to choose his intended drivers deliberately. Here's my theory. Maybe the phantom was 'hit' at that spot in the Roaring Twenties by a young man (twenty years old), but his body was hidden and never recovered. So he's reenacting his death scene over and over until someone finally searches and finds his long-lost remains. Then and only then will he lie down for the last time—not in the middle of the road in front of an approaching vehicle, but in the old Kendrew Corners Cemetery that's just across the bridge.

The Skeleton Ghost of Route 122

Constable

They were driving down Route 122 in the Town of Constable last year—a father, mother, and little girl—when the child, who'd been humming happy songs to herself, suddenly became silent. Her mother looked back at her daughter, just as the girl began to cry and squirm in her seat. Her eyes were wide with terror.

"Who was that near the road, Mommy?" she asked between sobs.

It was a clear, bitterly-cold North Country night, about twenty degrees below zero. There was no wind, and it was too cold to snow (something that makes sense to Northern New Yorkers). The three were on their way to the mall in Plattsburgh, and the parents had been carrying on a conversation in the front seat. They hadn't seen anything on the side of the road. But their daughter, who'd been so eager to get to the mall, was now begging to go back home. Her parents asked her what she saw, and she cried even harder, as if by talking about it, the horrid thing would come back. They tried to tell her it was nothing, but it was obvious that it was something. They'd never seen their daughter so frightened by anything before or since.

Again the mother asked the toddler gently what she'd seen, hoping to get enough details to say with sincerity that it was something perfectly harmless. But, to every honest attempt her parents made to offer a rational explanation for the sighting, the child responded with an insistence that it wasn't this, and it wasn't that.

It had been walking toward them on the left side of the road—whatever it was—and was tall, very, very tall. It was white and faceless, but it did have a head. It seemed like a person, because it was walking upright on two legs, but it wasn't wearing any clothes. Though they were on a rural stretch of road, the girl was adamant that it wasn't a horse or any other animal. She knew the difference. Strangely, she said you could see right through it, because it had holes all over it. In fact, she called it "that holy thing." Had she seen an apparition of a tall man? She was only three at the time and didn't know what a ghost even was, so she wouldn't have chosen that particular word to describe it. But she might have called such an image holy, for lack of a better description.

Then the questions started (and they haven't stopped to this day). She wanted to know why her parents hadn't seen it. Why was it there? Where did it come from? Who was it? Will it come back? Why was it 'so holy'? To every answer offered, an insistent "But, why?" followed. It's hard enough keeping up with a three-year-old's typical questions, without having a series of *impossible* questions spewed out—and with such great urgency.

Out of the blue one day this year, the little girl brought up the incident and referred to the apparition, if that's what it was, as "the big white skeleton" (now that she knows what a skeleton is). If *that's* what she saw, it makes sense that she originally said it had holes all over it that you could see through. Skeletons must look like that, through a child's eyes. Seeing a ghost in a three-piece suit would be bad enough, but seeing a scraggly *skeleton* ghost would be far worse, I would imagine.

The incident frightened the preschooler so much that even now, a full year later, she still recalls every detail of what she saw. When an older sibling asked her about it recently, she grew wide-eyed and choked up, as the unwanted memory flooded back. She whispered solemnly, "Don't ever go there." Pretty grim advice from one so small.

Next time you're passing through Constable on a cold winter's night, watch out for the "Skeleton Ghost" of Route 122!

The 'Thing'

South Colton

Peggy Neil West was thumbing through the photographs she'd just had developed and paused at the one of her daughter Scout. What a great picture—she's such a photogenic little girl. But what the heck was that white blob behind the weeds to Scout's right? That wasn't there when she took the photo. She was sure of it.

That's what they all say…when they discover a possible ghost in their photographs.

Photo by Peggy Neil West

White apparition to right of dog, South Colton

89

The land on which the photo was taken has been in the Neil family since the mid-1800s. Directly behind the weeds and the white blob in the photograph is the old Neil homestead, where Sirvillian Neil was born in 1850. Many years later, Peggy's grandmother died at the homestead of complications from cancer. Her body was dropped as it was removed from the house.

Peggy doesn't have a clue what the white "thing," as she calls it, could be. It doesn't look like a camera or film malfunction or processing error. And it doesn't look like any type of environmental interference. She said, "That picture has baffled me for over a year now." What she said next was typical of people everywhere who discover similar anomalies in their photographs.

"I didn't see anything with the naked eye when I took it. It was when we got the picture developed that we saw something more than Scout in the picture. The spot where the 'thing' presents itself is completely void of anything. There's only lawn there. There are no flowers or lawn ornaments—nothing! Directly in front of the 'thing' was once a favored aunt's vegetable garden." But it's all weeds now. Nothing else. Except, maybe...?

Peggy's sister-in-law, Nickie Neil, believes the anomaly looks like "a shape of either a tombstone or a head." I think it looks like a phantom scarecrow still guarding the defunct vegetable garden, or a classical ghost with sheet-over-its-head simplicity about to jump out of the weeds and say *boo*! It's that obvious.

Has Peggy or her family ever noticed anything unusual on the Neil property that would indicate the land might be haunted? Possibly. They've seen "weird fog from time to time" near the woods. They've heard unexplained noises and rustling in the bushes, and there have been times when felt like they were "not alone." But nothing has blatantly made itself known to them—until now, with this mysterious photograph.

One thing I've come to believe, having seen and heard much to base my opinion on, is that ghosts and spirits—if they really want to be seen—will *make* themselves seen. And they'll do so without your help, permission, or knowledge. This particular 'thing' clearly wanted to be seen—in all its glorious (albeit, undefined) splendor.

The Tree of Spirits

Jefferson County

The trees reflected in the river—they are unconscious of a spiritual world so near to them. So are we.

—Nathaniel Hawthorne (1804-1864)

I must say, it's been quite an ordeal bringing this book to fruition. The obstacles I've encountered during the writing process have almost become laughable. I had saved nearly my entire manuscript on a zip disk that went bad, and I lost all of my data. That was a good learning experience for me—always back up your saved projects! My laptop computer went on strike and refused to start working again. Some of the contributors had trouble sending or receiving correspondence related to their stories or photographs. It's just been one thing after the other. Suffice it to say, there are a lot of ghosts "dying to be seen" but apparently a handful that are not!

For example, I fell in love with the photograph below the first time I laid eyes on it at The Whispering Willow metaphysical shop and spiritual learning center in Sandy Creek. It was given to the owner of the business, Belle Salisbury, who placed the framed photograph in a prominent place on the wall in her office and dubbed it the "Tree of Spirits." If you look closely, there are many apparitions blending subtly into the background, especially beneath the lower branches and limbs. There are also a number of faces peeking out from behind tree limbs. The name is apt. As far as we know, the photograph was taken somewhere in Jefferson County. But the photographer who deserves credit for this gem of spirit photography is unknown.

The photograph was used in the Watertown Central School District's annual calendar for the 2002-2003 school year. It represented the month of August 2003. All of the photographs used in the annual calendar are carefully chosen from photographs taken by the previous year's photography students at Watertown Central High School, and the students' names are listed beneath their respective photographs. The August 2003 photograph is the only one without a name listed beneath it, so I called the school and asked if they knew who took the photograph of the magnificent tree. They have no idea; it wasn't one of their students. The school believes there was some sort of mix-up at the printer's (who I was unable, of course, to locate in Albany), because they inadvertently put the tree photo on the calendar in the slot designated for the August 2003 student photograph. Since it has already graced their public calendar anonymously, the school gave me permission to use the photograph, as long as I listed the photographer as 'unknown.'

So here it is—a mystery photo with a mysterious story behind it. Isn't she a beauty? See how many ghosts you can find in it. And if anyone knows who the photographer is, please let us know so he or she can be property acknowledged in future editions.

Photographer Unknown

The mysterious 'Tree of Spirits,' Jefferson County

The Union Hotel

Sackets Harbor

Seaway Trail Discovery Center in The Union Hotel, Sackets Harbor

The former Union Hotel, which is now the Seaway Trail Discovery Center, sits on the corner of Ray and West Main Streets and was built in 1817 by Frederick White, one of the wealthiest men in the North Country at that time. It's a Federal-style, three-story, limestone building that has aged remarkably well. Each floor of the museum is packed with interactive exhibits related to the Seaway Trail's attractions, territory, and history. The animatronic characters really bring the 1800s to life.

It's one of those places that everybody says is haunted, but few provide details. Usually, people approach me and simply say something like, "You should check out the Union Hotel in Sackets. Everyone knows that's haunted." So, I *knew* the Union Hotel was haunted two books ago, but I had to wait for someone with a little more substance to come along before I could include it in my writings. That someone came in the form of Miss Janis Monroe. Janis and her friend, Heather Montford, have visited the hotel-turned-museum several times, each time adding to their list of strange things that have happened to them while perusing the historic building's floors.

Not much happened to them the first or even the second time there, but the third time was definitely the charm for the inquisitive young ladies, and now they experience unexplained sensations every time they visit. Because it's located so close to the waterfront and the famous Sackets Harbor Battlefield, Janis and Heather feel that part of the reason they sense so much chaotic energy in the building is because so many soldiers lost their lives in the immediate vicinity. There are also rumors about the building that don't involve soldiers in battle nearby. One is that someone was buried long ago in the basement of the hotel. The other is that someone was taken to the attic in the mid-1800s in a secret meeting of a local service club and was never seen again. From its very foundation to its rooftop, the Union Hotel probably contains many secrets that were taken to just as many graves, adding a nice touch of mystery to the already enticing history of Sackets Harbor and the Seaway Trail. The best way to get a sense of the mystery one experiences there is, of course, to visit the museum yourself, as I did (my comments are sprinkled throughout this account). The next best way is to retrace Janis's and Heather's footsteps through the building on their most recent visit.

Upon entering the building, Janis and Heather didn't notice anything unusual. They went into the inviting gift shop to pay for their admission to the museum and walked down the hall to get into the comfortable, modern elevator that would take them to the third floor. You start at the top and work your way down. Walking down the hallway to the elevator, each woman had already begun to feel a bit dizzy and noticed that the air around them seemed to be getting heavier. Being on the elevator intensified the feeling, and stepping off didn't end it. (See the photograph below of at least two orbs that greeted me as I stepped off the elevator on the third floor.) A mass of thick air seemed to surround them, even as they entered the orientation room. Native birds and plants were painted across the walls, and the floors were painted a vibrant blue. But the whimsical, outdoorsy setting was in stark contrast to the oppressive sensation the women experienced there.

Photo by Author

Orbs on third floor of Seaway Trail Discovery Center, Sackets Harbor

The description Janis offered reminded me of a fun house or horror house you'd go into at a fair. She said, "The floor we walked on seemed uneven, like we were walking on waves, and every so often we passed through 'hot spots' of energy that seemed to move. With one step we were fine, and with the next, we were caught in a grip of heart-racing, body-buzzing sensations." *This is one ride that's definitely worth the ticket price!*

When I visited the museum with my youngest, she giggled and said, "Whoa, the floor feels like it's moving!" The floor may have a slight wave to it in some places, like floors of such old buildings often do—so you might feel like you're a bit off balance in those areas. I just thought it was interesting that my daughter described it exactly as Janis had.

In the orientation room, Janis got a psychic impression of a group of people around a table all conversing about something important. She felt like they were being stared at. What's interesting is that she had no idea that the third floor had been a meeting hall for the Masons in the 1800s. When she told me about her visit to the museum, she said, "Ever since that visit, I've wondered if that was a meeting room of some sort." And, until she reads the draft of this story, she *still* doesn't know that her impression of that room that day was probably very accurate. I only found out it had been a meeting room after Janis had shared her experiences with me, when I was looking for historical background for the story. (My youngest daughter loved the whole museum, but she especially enjoyed the Seaway Trail cars in the orientation room—and apparently she wasn't the only one who enjoyed them! See the photo below.)

Photo by Author

Orb in Orientation Room, Seaway Trail Discovery Center, Sackets Harbor

The next room Janis and Heather entered had been a ballroom in its day. Janis said that, although there was a lot of energy there, it was more pleasant and less intense than in the orientation room. Other than that, the rest of the third floor was supernaturally unremarkable, so the women took the stairs down to the second floor. They did notice that the stairs themselves gave off interesting vibes. As they made their way down, they lost their balance or felt like they would several times. (When I visited, I found the new stairs to be very safe and sound. The old, original stairs are roped off and no longer used. The building has been beautifully modernized to meet code but still retains its historic flavor.)

The second floor proved to be the most interesting for Janis and Heather. In fact, Janis said it's usually the worst floor for her—which is a good thing if you're looking for what she was looking for, which is a genuine haunted building. She immediately felt that she and Heather were "once again among spirits" in a room full of artifacts like swords, military uniforms, a long wooden box possibly used to store guns in, items found on old ships, and more. She said, "Both of us had a hard time walking by the uniforms, and all I could think was that they were going to break out of their casings and grab me!" In such a historical place, she reasoned, anything was possible.

Just as on the third floor, Janis again felt like they were being watched, only this time, not from a safe distance. As they stood before the long wooden box, she felt as though they were surrounded by male spirits, and at least one was right in her face. "His face was right next to mine. I wasn't cold, but warm, like he was breathing on me. I wanted to shove him away, but I knew I couldn't. Still, I stepped closer to the box, and Heather did the same. We wanted to touch it to see if we could get any impressions from it. I had the hardest time getting my hand close enough to it. It felt like there was a force field around it. When I finally did touch it, I didn't feel much."

The ladies stood transfixed at the box for a few more moments, when all of a sudden, they both felt the floor beneath them give way at the very same time. Both grabbed the wooden railing in front of them simultaneously to regain their balance before leaving the room. The male ghost Janis felt next to her face remained in the room behind them. "It was like he was bound to that room and was pulled away from me when I left," she said. And good riddance!

The kitchen on the first floor was the next stop. This, too, was a highly "energized" room, but its atmosphere was much better. It was the "happiest" room. Janis and Heather each took turns standing in front of the brick oven and fireplace to see what they sensed. Janice's impression was of a woman working there wearing old-fashioned clothing. When she gets impressions like this, she said, "I feel like I'm there in the past for a moment and then spontaneously return." Both women felt "bursts of activity" in different areas of the kitchen, leading them to believe that it's a very active room, as far as ghosts go.

Off the kitchen is a small room with a gigantic animatronic cow (another favorite of both young and old). Though the talking cow, sitting up with its legs crossed, is very engaging as it tells you about the local dairy industry, Janis and Heather's attention was drawn to the door to the right of the cow. (Somehow, I completely missed the door, and I was probably leaning right up against it! I must have been too engrossed in the cow's presentation.) Heather, who was standing right behind Janis, whispered to her friend that there was something hot behind that door—meaning hot spirit energy. Janis's first reaction was to back away, but then she lifted her hand toward the door, and, to her surprise, she found that she couldn't touch it. But she didn't have to touch it to feel the heat emanating from it. Both women fear that whatever—or whomever—was behind that door was worse than anything else they had felt the whole time they were there, or any of the times they had ever been there, for that matter.

It's just as well that Janis couldn't bring herself to touch the door, whether it was her own fear preventing her from further investigating what lie beyond, or it was a force field created by a spirit hell-bent on keeping intruders out. There will be other visits, though, and sooner or later, Janis will get through to the other side—after all, isn't that what this is all about, getting through to the "Other Side"?

Underground Neighbors

Adams Center

I believe that if I should die,
And you were to walk near my grave,
From the very depths of the earth,
I would hear your footsteps.

—Benito Perez Galdos (1843-1920)

When Bud and Bev Perry bought the old brick house on Route 11 in 1978, they didn't mind that their home was adjacent to the Union Cemetery. In fact, it was only four feet from the cemetery on one side; and the fence in their backyard was all that came between their yard and the cemetery. But the real estate agent and former owners sort of forgot to tell them that the man who built the house, Jay Harmon, was buried in that very cemetery, and his burial plot was right up against the fence in their backyard. Oh, and one more thing…Mr. Harmon had been found dead in his bed, in the Perry's house. That's not to say that Mr. Harmon now haunts the Perry home. Indeed, it could be any one of the slew of people lying six feet under on surrounding property. But clearly some-one has haunted it for the last twenty years.

The first time anything happened was actually several years after the Perrys moved in. Bud went downstairs to the kitchen one morning and found that the oven in his electric stove was turned on. Over the next two decades, lights turned on in the middle of the night, and television sets came on full blast between two and three o'clock in the morning, including two sets that could only be manually-operated. The last time it happened, one television came on by itself two nights in a row at the same time, so the Perrys now keep it unplugged at night. Each time that they've bought new sets, they've given away the old ones; and the new owners of those sets have never experienced any problems with them in *their* homes. It was just something about the Perry residence that made them act up.

The Perrys have twins sons (now grown), Dave and Dan. About twelve years ago, Bud and Bev were getting ready to go to bed when Dave came in and told them he heard someone making noise in their driveway. He said it sounded like someone shoveling snow on the concrete driveway, but it was July. Bud went to his bedroom window to look out into the backyard. Where four white, plastic chairs were positioned in a semicircle, he saw about fifty small, white lights "hovering and dancing up and down above the chairs." They were not fireflies; nothing like that. But they may have been orbs from the cemetery partying it up. They say the grass is always greener on the other side of the fence, right? Bud shook his head and rubbed his eyes, but the orbs were still there for at least another minute before disappearing (they must have realized they'd been busted). The surreal experience seemed to shift Bud into a trance-like mode while it was happening, because he couldn't look away—or get his wits about him—long enough to tell his wife and son to look out the window and see what was going on. Many people find paranormal experiences like this to be so dreamlike that they don't react the way they would have expected themselves to react if they'd been in their normal state of mind. It's a common finding for those who've unwittingly entered the 'Twilight Zone.'

Besides the ghost with the appliance fetish and the ghosts involved in the phantasmal disco dance in the backyard, the Perrys also believe they've been visited by the spirit of their beloved dog, Patches. The 'old girl' lived to be nearly eighteen years old and died in 2001. Their other dog, Molly, is three years old. Bud said, "Last year my wife heard a dog crying on two occasions and did not tell me. Then one morning, I heard the crying downstairs close to me. But Molly was upstairs fast asleep, and my wife was online!" The Perrys believe that Patches was upset because they had just installed new carpet, and Patches had loved the old carpet that had her scent on it.

When Patches died, Bud built a fire in their yard and cremated her, then respectfully spread her ashes around the cemetery where he and Patches had taken so many enjoyable walks together. He now worries that she's not content on the other side, because she seems to return from time to time. It's the only happening in the house that has upset him, because they loved her so much, and they only want her to be at peace. They needn't worry. Our pets and loved ones often return to visit us once in a while, simply because they love us so much, but they don't stay long. They just come and go whenever the mood strikes. They have other places to go and things to do. We may feel them (i.e. the breeze from their wagging tails) or hear them bark or meow or chirp, or we may just sense they are there because there was something unique they did when alive, and it still seems to happen sometimes. Like the cat that kept scratching at her master's bedroom door and the dog whose wagging tail kept shaking the Christmas tree ornaments long after he'd passed away. Patches is fine.

The month of February is particularly active for the ghost or spirit that haunts the Perry house, possibly because that's the month Jay Harmon died in. Several times, the Perrys heard voices, but they couldn't understand what was being said or determine exactly where the voices were coming from. Relatives spending the night have heard footsteps going up and down the stairs when nobody was there; and the family's cat and dogs have all stopped and stared at a chair near their front window, for no apparent reason. Objects fall off the shelves and walls, and Bud has felt what he thought was Molly walk up behind him, only to find the dog wasn't there.

When their son Dan was young, he thought they should move. But now, as an adult, he just laughs about it. It's a typical haunted home. There's nothing threatening…and certainly nothing worth moving over. Most people, in fact, who live in haunted homes don't move out on account of it, because the vast majority of hauntings are harmless.

Wings

Plattsburgh

Angels and ministers of grace defend us.

—William Shakespeare's Hamlet

Three days before Thanksgiving 2003, Amanda Armstrong was taking a shower when she suddenly felt a little faint. The eighteen-year-old college freshman stepped out of the tub and sat down, but when she stood up again, she passed out and cracked the back of her skull in the fall. The bleeding caused a subdural hematoma—a blood clot in the front of her brain. She was taken to Fletcher Allen Medical Center in Burlington for treatment and observation. A month later, her neurosurgeon was amazed at her rapid recovery. It was as if someone 'up there' was watching over her.

Indeed, someone was, and Amanda has the photographs to prove it!

Like all teenagers, Amanda and her friends take lots of photographs of their immediate circle of friends clumped together in heaping piles of smiles. Three photographs that were taken recently in a dorm room on the SUNY Plattsburgh campus revealed something truly remarkable—and wonderfully ethereal. Do you believe in angels?

In the first photograph that was taken by Jared Greene, Amanda is reclining against the wall with her fingers combing through her hair, unaware that she has incoming company. To her left is Lauren Mulvaugh, and to her right are Hillary Littlejohn and Noah Flint. Just above and to the left of Amanda's head is a white, teardrop-shaped splotch against the backdrop of a paper wall calendar. It doesn't appear to be a film flaw or lens reflection. In fact, had it been a reflection off an object in the background, it wouldn't cut in front of a portion of her upper scalp, as it does in the second photo. There are no other such abnormalities in the entire photograph. Interestingly, the photographs taken just before and after this one (and the next) came out blank when they were developed.

Photo by Jared Greene

Angel coming in for a landing? Plattsburgh

The next two photographs taken of Amanda and her friends that day were similar to the one above, except the white splotch settled in and made itself comfortable right on top of Amanda's head! Notice the perfect angel shape-wings, upper torso, and head? The glorious brilliance of the little being is also an indication of its divine nature. Most people immediately think it's an angel—especially when they look back at the first photograph again. Doesn't the first one look like an angel in profile coming in for a landing? As is usually the case with paranormal photography, the photographer didn't see anything like this when he took the pictures.

There are a couple of other things that might explain Amanda's mys-

Photo by Jared Greene

Angel, ghost, or Thor? Plattsburgh

terious companion, if it's not an angel. Her dearly loved dog whose name was Charlie Thor passed away. He was called Thor for short. In Nordic mythology, Thor was known as "The Thunder God," and he is often depicted in comic books and fantasy art as a striking, red-haired Viking wearing a silver cap with gold wings clipped to the sides. Was Amanda's dog, Thor, presenting himself as the Norse God who was his namesake to make it more obvious who he was? It wouldn't be the first time a deceased pet has come back to visit its owners. Many people believe they've seen, heard, or felt the presence of beloved pets that passed away.

Perhaps more plausibly, it was photographic evidence of a visitation by one of Amanda's grandfathers—both of whom passed away within the last five years. Or maybe it's an unknown ghost ham that simply wanted to be included in the group photo. After all, SUNY Plattsburgh has its share of stories about ghosts roaming the halls, just as campuses all the world over do. Personally, I think it's an angel—it looks pretty straight forward and makes sense. I'd certainly love to believe that's what it is.

Conclusion

People who lean on logic and philosophy and rational exposition end by starving the best part of their mind.

—William Butler Yeats (1865-1939)

It's important to understand that a lot of unexplained things can show up on film, and you've seen a good assortment of examples in this book. But not every photographic anomaly is a ghost—per se. That's the part I want to underscore. The spirit world consists of far more than just ghosts. People have taken photographs of beautiful spirit energy they believe is divine in nature (angels, spirit guides, deceased loved ones, Virgin Mary and Christ apparitions, and so on). The possibilities are limitless, if you have an open mind.

Ghost pictures are thrilling and wonderfully creepy, bridging time and connecting us to the past. Pictures of a divine nature are uplifting and mystical, bringing us hope and a much-needed sense of security. They connect us to Heaven, and to our future. But, no matter what their nature, all photographs of spirit energy remind us that we're not alone. We're being watched, and we're being watched over.

There's a whole unseen world around us of beings that are 'dying to be seen,' if we would only trust our senses and first impressions and actually believe what we see when it's staring us straight in the face. They present themselves to us in many ways under many guises, and they all have something to teach us about our past, present, or future.

107

Some give us a glimpse of how it used to be, to remind us of where we came from. Some let us know they are here, watching over us at this very moment. And some bring us face to face with our own immortality. If you believe in them—in ghosts and spirits and angels and loved ones communicating with us from beyond—then you must know that we go on...

Forever.

All Is Well

"Death is nothing at all. I have only slipped away into the next room. I am I, and you are you. Whatever we were to each other, that we still are. Call me by my old familiar name, speak to me in the easy way which you always used. Put no difference in your tone, wear no forced air of solemnity or sorrow. Laugh as we always laughed at the little jokes we enjoyed together. Play, smile, think of me, pray for me. Let my name be ever the household word that it always was; let it be spoken without effect, without a trace of a shadow on it. Life means all that it ever meant. It is the same as it ever was; there is unbroken continuity. Why should I be out of mind because I am out of sight? I am waiting for you, for an interval, somewhere very near, just 'round the corner. All is well."

—Henry Scott Holland (1847-1918)

Bibliography

Cady, Anne M. "Index to 1865 Beer's Atlas for St. Lawrence County, New York." Translated by Mary Woodman. Index of A. Cady's Online Genealogy Transcription Data. (2004) http://freepages.genealogy.rootswell.com/~stlawgen/MISC/Beers/Beersatl.htm

Cady, Anne M. "1870 Census of Massena, St. Lawrence County, p. 555A." *Index of A. Cady's Online Genealogy Transcription Data.* (2004) http://freepages.genealogy.rootswell.com/~stlawgen/index.htm

Curtis, Gates, ed. *History of St. Lawrence County, New York.* Syracuse, N.Y.: D. Mason & Company, 1894.

Fuller, Joyce. *Ft. Jackson Putnam to Sylvester.* http://freepages.genealogy. rootsweb.com/~slccemeteries/Hopkinton/ft_jackson_intro.htm Mar. 2004

The Heuvelton Bee, 1902. (No further bibliographical information available.)

Hornack, Paul. "Hoover Inn's New Operator Inherits 174 Years of History and a Ghost." *Watertown Daily Times*, 8 Dec. 2002: B3.

Hough, Franklin B. "War of 1812." *History of St. Lawrence and Franklin Counties.* 1852.

"Recalls Early Massena Days." *Massena Observer*, 20 Aug. 1936: Sec. 2, 1.

Seaway Trail Discover Center. (2002-2004). http://www.seawaytrail.com

Weber, Richard E. and Sprague, A. Arnold. "Dr. Gideon Sprague & Maria Pier." (Mar. 2004). http://www.sprague-database.org/02-04/f8743.htm

Young, Holice B. "LeRay, Jefferson, NY, Evans' Mills." (Dec. 1999). http://www.usgennet.org/usa/ny/county/jefferson/leray/leevans.htm

About the Author

Photo by Creative Imaging

Author Cheri Revai

Cheri Revai is the best-selling author of *Haunted Northern New York* (2002), *More Haunted Northern New York* (2003), and *Haunted Massachusetts: Ghosts and Strange Phenomena of the Bay State* (Stackpole Books, July 2005). She writes regional non-fiction pieces dealing with mysterious, historical, and/or paranormal topics and has appeared on television and radio programs throughout New York State.

Revai, a North Country native, lives in St. Lawrence County with her husband and her four daughters. You may write to her at P.O. Box 295, Massena, NY 13662, or send e-mail to: hauntedny@yahoo.com. The *Haunted Northern New York* companion website is www.hauntedny.com.